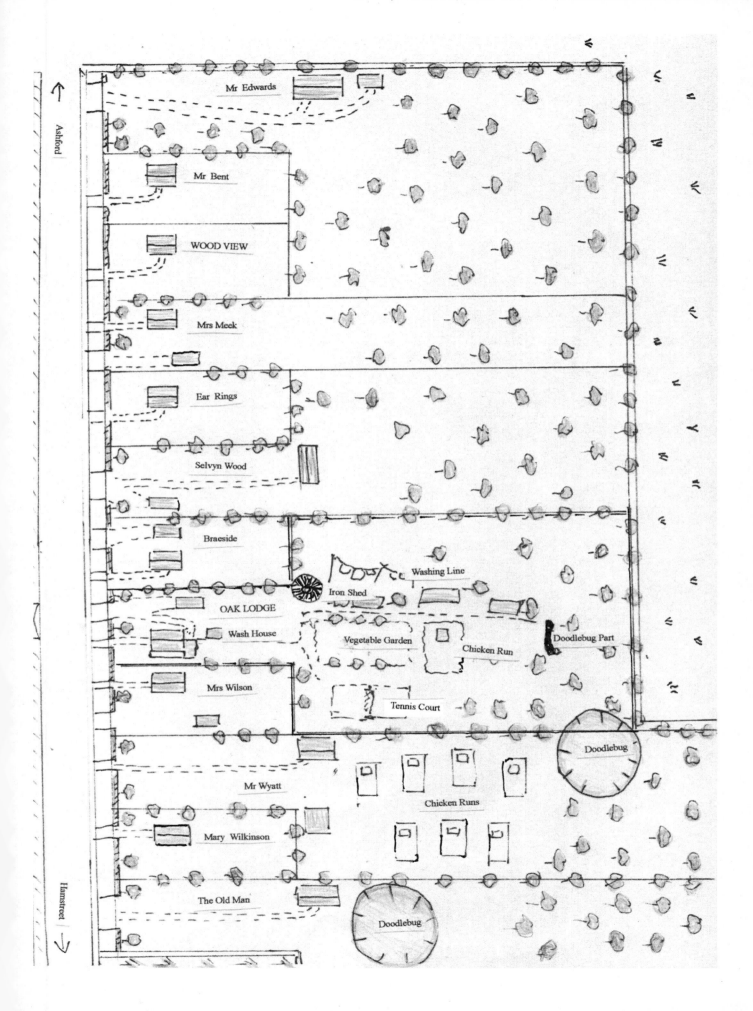

About the Author

Avril is in her eighties, and has enjoyed reading books all of her life. She believes that those of us who enjoy reading books should write one, and this is hers.

Dedication

This book is dedicated to my brother, John Walker, growing up in the war years would not have been the same without him.

Avril Easton

A WAR TIME CHILDHOOD AND THIS IS THE WAY I SAW IT

AUSTIN MACAULEY PUBLISHERS™
LONDON • CAMBRIDGE • NEW YORK • SHARJAH

A CIP catalogue record for this title is available from the British Library.

ISBN 9781398424302 (Paperback)
ISBN 9781398424319 (Hardback)
ISBN 9781398424326 (ePub e-book)

www.austinmacauley.com

First Published (2021)
Austin Macauley Publishers Ltd
25 Canada Square
Canary Wharf
London
E14 5LQ

Chapter 1

John and Me with Rags and Kitty Wee.

As a child growing up during the Second World War, family members over the generations have often asked me about my memories of that time. This is how I remember it.

The war started in 1939 while I was in my first year at the Primary School and ended in 1945, during my first year at the Grammar School. I have fewer, fainter memories of my childhood before the war, than during and after the war and they seemed to be very happy years. I was born on 14th November 1933, 1 year and 11 days after my brother, John, was born on 3rd November 1932. We were both born at Oak Lodge, a wooden bungalow in the middle of a row of assorted detached bungalows, surrounded by woods, forests and fields, most of which belonged to Harden's farm situated further along the main Ashford to Hastings road in the Parish of Orlestone. The market town of Ashford was four and a half miles to the north and the nearest village, Hamstreet, was two miles to the south. There was a small general store with a Post Office and a telephone box about a mile towards Ashford. Hamstreet was our main shopping centre, with a grocer, a butcher, a baker, a green grocer, a shoe mender, an iron monger, the doctor's surgery, the main post office and Tippens Garage.

The Dukes Head Public House was in the centre of the village, and on the outskirts was the railway station, next to the Church Hall and opposite the village school.

Our bungalow stood near the road in four and a half acres of land, about one third woodland, and one third rough grassland with the occasional large oak tree. Before the war, this was where most of the animals were kept. We had about two to three hundred chickens in houses and pens, ducks in a pen with a pond, a few goats in a shed; these were chained to trees in daytime, and rabbits in rows of double decker hutches; some outside and some inside another shed. On the rest of the land were huge vegetable gardens edged with fruit trees and lawns surrounded with many flower beds. Near the house were even more sheds for various uses. The 'Iron Shed', a round tent like, World War 1 army hut, made of corrugated iron and painted black, was where, in the winter, trees were sawn into logs and stored to keep dry. Potatoes were also stored there in a bunker made of old railway sleepers, sacks and straw. An assortment of garden tools were also kept there, some quite dangerous, and a large wooden wheelbarrow my father had built. One morning my father went into the Iron Shed to get this wheelbarrow and as he opened the iron shed's door, the blackened shape of the wheelbarrow collapsed into a pile of ashes, leaving the wheel intact. He was always lighting bonfires and a spark must have landed in the wheelbarrow and gradually turned the wood into charcoal overnight. Nothing else in the shed was damaged. He rebuilt the wheelbarrow using the original wheel and it lasted for the rest of his life. Nearer to the house was 'The Wash-house', with a built-in copper which had its own fire box and chimney. The large steel bowl in the centre was filled with rain water from the water butts and heated with sticks from the wood; this was the only way to heat enough water for washing clothes or to fill the tin bath. The tin bath was kept in the wash house as well as the iron mangle with wooden rollers and an assortment of bowls and buckets. There was a garage with adjoining workshops containing more tools, a spacious wood store and a big coal bunker.

Before the war, my father was an Insurance Agent and would go off to work most days on his bicycle. He covered quite a large area and would visit my maternal Grandmother in Folkestone, about twenty miles away, for dinner once a week. We had a dog called 'Rags', a black, brown and white curly coated mongrel with a split nose, due to having gotten too close to the scythe my father was using. I remember my father picking him up and throwing him, for fun, and he would come back, leap into my father's arms to be thrown again. We had a tabby Manx tailless cat, called Kitty Wee, who was always having kittens. As soon as the kittens were born, our mother would select one (with a tail), for the cat to keep and put the rest in a bucket of water, then push down another bucket on top, to drown them.

Each week our mother killed some of the chickens, by ringing their necks, then plucking and preparing them for sale at Ashford market. Rags would devotedly guard these dead chickens, but I cannot remember him guarding them when they were alive. In later years my mother told me that my father did not like killing the animals, so, if she could not kill them, he would no longer keep them. I would help my mother collect the eggs from the nesting boxes at the back of the chicken houses; these were wiped clean with a damp cloth and placed in cardboard egg trays which were packed into large yellow wooden crates, which were picked up once a week by the Egg man in his large van.

When my father was at home, he was always busy. He would be working in the garden, looking after the animals, building sheds, moving chicken runs, chopping down trees, sawing logs, or in the greenhouse growing plants. My father never did any housework. My mother was always at home, looking after us, cooking and doing the housework. She also looked after the animals while my father was at work and helped in the garden. Although my parents had very little spare time, we went for cycle rides around the countryside, me sitting in a seat on the back of my mother's bicycle and my brother sitting on a little seat on the crossbar of my father's bicycle. On one occasion, we visited the Hill family who lived on Hamstreet Hill. Just before the war, they moved to a house on Sugarloaf Crossroads where Mr Hill looked after the horses for Hardens Farm and the daughter, Doris, became a friend of mine. This must have happened before Valerie and Lesley were born.

Family and friends came to stay for holidays. Rather strangely, my father's parents would come to stay separately, never together. I liked my grandmother but disliked my grandfather, I do not know why! We called him 'Pa'. Auntie Vi, my mother's only sister, came to stay quite often, sometimes with her husband, Uncle Manuel, who was a sailor on H.M.S. Neptune. He called my aunt 'Vidy' although her name was really Violet. Because my mother was very fair, with pale blue eyes, my grandmother named her Lily and her sister was named Violet because she had dark hair and dark eyes; I was told. I have a very happy memory of being at the seaside, sitting on the beach with Uncle Manuel, looking at the sea. I cannot remember where we were or who else was there. The only other time I can remember going to a seaside before the war, was with the whole family, to Camber Sands, in Uncle Laurie's car. It was very windy and the sand stung my eyes. Uncle Laurie, who lived in Yorkshire, was a friend of my father, and came to stay with us regularly, as he had a business supplying shops with seaside picture postcards in most of the coastal towns nearby. Very occasionally, his wife came and once they brought their son, Trevor, who was about the same age as Valerie.

When my sister, Valerie, arrived in August 1937, the District Nurse told my brother and me that a stork had brought her! Occasionally my brother and I were allowed to watch her being bathed by the District Nurse. In my parents' bedroom was a washstand on which stood a large bowl, a large jug and a matching soap dish. The kettle was boiled in the kitchen and taken with the jug of cold water to the bedroom. The waters were poured into the bowl and the temperature was tested by the nurse with her elbow before the baby was bathed, dried, powdered and dressed. My mother and the baby were supposed to stay in the bedroom for two weeks but I think she was far too busy for that.

Not long after my sister, Valerie, was born, my father had a serious accident. One dark night, with his coat thrown over his pyjamas, he went looking for Rags and was knocked off his bike by a van, and ended up in hospital with a broken shoulder blade. It had been important to find the missing dog because there was a foot and mouth epidemic at that time and farmers were shooting dogs on sight to help prevent the disease from spreading. When our mother visited my father in hospital, she left us with Mrs Wilson, the lady next door. We sat in her garden, having tea surrounded by roses and other beautiful flowers. I remember sneaking into that garden to pick tulips to press the petals between the pages of books. It was the only garden around were tulips grew and they are still one of my favourite flowers. After the injury had healed, my father still could not lift his arm up. Then, Uncle Laurie came to stay and my father started walking around with his arm up in the air. Apparently, Uncle Laurie was a hypnotist, and he hypnotised my father and cured his arm. Although a significant part of his shoulder blade was missing, my father spent the rest of his life working extremely hard, even joining the army, with no problems at all. About the same time, my mother and I noticed that I had developed a lazy eye, and she asked Uncle Laurie if he could correct the disorder using hypnosis. She was told, unfortunately not, since children could not be hypnotised. Around the same time, John and I went into hospital to have our tonsils out; he was put in a bed in the men's ward and I was put in a cot in the children's ward. In the theatre, a mask was put over my face, and I still have a strange memory of myself in the corner of the ceiling, looking down at myself on the operating table! After a few days, our mother came and took my brother home from hospital but left me there. I was not happy, but eventually Mrs Wilson came and took me home.

The last Christmas before the war started, my father took John and me to London on the train, to visit our grandparents, aunts, uncles and cousins. We took some of our chickens for their Christmas dinners. We stayed in a big house in Richmond Road, Hackney, with steps going down to a front door and steps going up to another front door. We went into the house through the downstairs door, down a very long passage to a big kitchen with a very colourful dresser along one wall. The only toilet was outside, which was strange to us, because ours, at home, was indoors. This house was bombed at the beginning of the war and my Grandparents moved to a house in Eltham. The Christmas lights and shop windows in London were amazing. We went to Selfridge's to see Father Christmas, I had only seen him once before, at a party, in the vicarage, where we had played hunt the slipper. The Selfridge's Father Christmas sat on a throne, at the top of a huge flight of stairs, surrounded by elves, Christmas trees covered in lights and a huge pile of presents. My brother went first and got a present, a blow football game, I think. I went up the stairs next and Father Christmas gave me a huge box wrapped in Christmas paper. My parcel was three times the size of my brother's parcel. I opened my present and it was magical; full of small, sparkling, coloured balls in beautiful colours: red, green, blue, yellow, purple, silver and gold; each colour in individual compartments surrounding a raised square piece of cardboard with holes in it. The idea was to make patterns with the coloured beads. As there were to be very few toys available during the war years, these beads were played with so much, the sparkle wore off, and many were trodden on and crushed to a red powder. I do not remember coming back from London on the train, but I do remember coming home from the station on the bus with the box of beads on my lap. On the same trip to London, Auntie Elsie, my father's sister, who had no children of her own, took John and me to the Hackney Empire Theatre. I have no memory of the production but I do remember having tea in the interval. A small table was attached to the side of the seat and a tray was brought with a teapot, milk jug, sugar bowl, water jug and a plate of cakes. I was told later that children were only allowed to go to afternoon shows. This was my only visit to the theatre until long after the war. One Christmas, before the war, my father built me a lovely dolls' house with lights powered by a torch battery hidden in the roof; he made all the furniture and my mother made the curtains and soft furnishings. I cannot remember what became of that dolls' house.

Before the war, the only hint we had that Christmas was coming, was the postman bringing Christmas cards, which we opened and displayed on the mantel piece. I loved these cards because most of them had coloured ribbons or silky tassels on them. We had a front room in our house, a room we seldom went in, particularly in the winter, as it was very cold, but when we woke up on Christmas morning, that room had been transformed with a blazing log fire, a big Christmas tree in one corner with baubles and lights and presents underneath. Decorations had been put up around the room and there was a bowl of assorted nuts with nut crackers on the top and a large bowl of fruit: apples, oranges, pears, bananas and tangerines. But, there were no grapes (when I was a child, grapes were only given to sick people).

One Easter, before the war, I received a particularly lovely present from the relations in London. In the parcel, delivered by the postman, was a box containing an Easter egg in a beautiful royal gold coach, made of cardboard, drawn by six celluloid white horses. Other toys I played with included a little cut out cardboard thatched cottage, a miniature copy of the play house of the Royal princesses, and a cardboard figure of Shirley Temple (a famous child movie star) with lots of cut out paper clothes that fitted on the figure with tabs. I also had a celluloid doll with a hole in her celluloid hair to fix a ribbon in. This doll came to a sad end, as somehow it got too near the fire and went up in a sheet of flames, inside the fire guard, and disappeared to nothing. I think my brother was involved somehow, because our mother slapped him. Because all the other dolls I had before the war were made of china, they were easily broken. As we had no new dolls during the war, my mother mended them for my sisters to play with, until they were beyond repair.

Although I have no recollection of this, I must have begun my school life in the Autumn Term of 1938, when I was five years old. We were picked up outside our bungalow by a little green school bus; we called 'The Tub'. It went round the lanes, picking up children along the way. We were the only children living on the main road and were picked up last in the morning and dropped off last in the afternoon. Before the war, I cannot remember the clothes I wore, or what we ate for breakfast, dinner or tea, but I can remember very happy, sunny days with my brother, mother, father and the babies. During my childhood, all tradesmen came to our house. Mr Harden, the local farmer was also the milkman and came every morning, including Sundays, with a churn of milk. The milk was measured with a pint and a half pint dipper into jugs supplied by my mother. The baker came with a big wicker basket full of loaves, about three times a week. I cannot recall if there were any buns or cakes in the basket but there was only one type of bread during the war which was wholemeal, this was not rationed until after the war. The butcher came twice a week, delivering the order made on his previous visit, collecting the money and the order for the next delivery. Sometimes he would bring 'lights' (lungs) wrapped in brown paper, for the dog and cat. The grocer came, on his bicycle, once a week to collect the money, coupons and the order book where my mother had written the list of the groceries she wanted. These were delivered by van later in the week. A fisherman came, about once a week, in a little three wheeled van, with the fresh fish he had caught earlier that day. Occasionally an ice cream man came, selling ice lollies, in triangular cardboard tubes; they tasted lovely, a real treat. The man in a big green van delivered paraffin and candles and the man covered in coal dust came in a lorry to deliver coal. I can remember being told, by my mother, to count the sacks as they were being emptied into the coal bunker. Coal was rationed during the war and I usually counted twenty sacks.

Living in the country, there were no pavements, no street lights, no dustman and we had to dispose of all our own rubbish. A 'Rag and Bone Man' would occasionally pass by with a horse and cart, to pick up clothes, old beds, bottles, tins and anything else that was difficult to dispose of, or had any value or further use. Gypsies would knock on the door, selling heather or primroses in season, and pegs made of wood with a metal band made from old tin cans holding them together. These were the only pegs my mother used to hang the washing on the line. These pegs became rusty and marked the clothes if they got wet so my mother was always careful to keep them dry. The washing line was a simple length of rope, suspended between two trees, just high enough to hang the washing on. The rope with the washing on was then lifted higher with a prop, a tall wooden pole with a forked end. Mondays were wash days and our mother would always do this in the wash house. All the clothes were washed by hand, but the cotton sheets, towels, nappies and anything else that was cotton and white, were boiled in the copper. The copper needed piles of sticks to fuel the fire, to heat the water; we children often helped collect the right sized sticks from the wood at the bottom of the garden. The wash-house also doubled as the bath-house. Once a week, we all had a bath in the wash-house during the summer months and in the kitchen during the winter months. The copper was filled with rain water from the water butts and the fire was lit and maintained with sticks from the wood. From the youngest to the oldest, we took our turns to bathe. Initially the bath was filled with clean, hot water from the copper, and then additional hot water was added for the next person, so the last person had the deepest bath, with well used water. I enjoyed bath time in the wash-house, the red glow of the wood fire in the copper, the warm steamy air and the smell of wood smoke. It was not so enjoyable bathing in the kitchen in the winter. Hair was always washed at the kitchen sink, in rain water, heated on the stove. One packet of 'Eve' shampoo powder mixed with water in a mug was used to wash everybody's hair.

Sunday evening was bath night, and then we had clean pyjamas and clean clothes for school the next morning. As the war progressed, we out grew nightwear and it was not replaced until after the war, so we went to bed in our vest and knickers.

One sunny day, dressed in our best clothes, we were told that a famous person would be driving by and we were to wave to them. Mrs Wilson, from next door, put a garden seat outside her house, on the edge of the road. We sat and waited for hours and hours, but I have no memory of waving to a famous person. Then the war started and there were no lit windows, no street lights, no lit shop windows, no Christmas lights, no more trips to London, so the memory of these things had to last me for at least the next five years. And the first top shop in Ashford opened after I left school.

Me with my present from Father Christmas.

Mummy, Daddy, Uncle Manuel, John and Avril at the seaside

Auntie Vi, John and Avril at Oak Lodge before the war

Nanna Walker, Mummy, John, Avril and Nancy

Summer 1934. Daddy, Mummy, John and Avril at Oak Lodge

Auntie Vi, John and Avril at Oak Lodge with Nancy. The goat that was given to the Goat Woman.

19

Chapter 2

Me ready for school.

Nineteen-thirty-nine was the year that changed all our lives. My second youngest sister, Lesley, was born in the June. This time the District Nurse told us that she brought the baby in her black bag! World War II broke out in the September and my father left home to join the army. I had my eyes tested and started wearing my first pair of glasses. Before this time I cannot remember every wandering out of our garden and woods, but by now, John and I were older and becoming more adventurous, began exploring the surrounding countryside. This worried my mother but she said we always came back when we were hungry.

When Lesley was born, John and I stood at the front gate shouting, "We have a new baby sister". Auntie Vi came to stay from Folkestone, bringing with her, one-year-old, Michael, which made three little ones in the house. She brought with her a lovely Silver-Cross pram which she left behind with my mother when she returned home. This was because Michael screamed every time he was put in it, so she bought a smaller pram for him. We often went for walks with this posh pram, with the two toddlers sitting on seats at each end, with their feet in the foot well in the middle.

This was the year I was taken to an eye specialist at Maidstone Hospital, where there was a machine where I was told to put the lion in the cage. I ended up wearing glasses with a patch over one eye. I mainly only wore these glasses to school as I could see perfectly well without them. Very often on school mornings, it was a hunt for the lost glasses before the bus came.

The actual outbreak of war was not memorable, nor my father's enlisting, but I do remember him coming home on leave for the first time. When my father joined the Royal Artillery Regiment, at the beginning of the war, he told my mother that if he joined early, rather than being conscripted, he would get a better position. That year my father was thirty four years old, and my mother, at twenty seven, was living in the country, virtually a single parent with four children aged six, five, two and a baby of three months. He was probably right to join the army early, because he was posted around England, and never went abroad until D-day in 1944, which meant he came home on leave two or three times a year. I remember my father coming in the door for the first time dressed as a soldier, he was wearing a peeked hat with a brass badge of a gun on the front, a jacket with brass buttons down the front, a leather belt with a brass buckle, and black shiny boots. He also had with him, a big heavy khaki overcoat, a tin hat, a gas mask, a kit bag and a gun. He showed us, in his kit bag, a sewing kit, a shoe polishing kit and a brass cleaning kit with a gadget which enabled buttons to be polished without spoiling the cloth beneath. 1519608 was the number on one of the two discs he wore on a cord round his neck, one red, and the other beige.

What happened to all the chickens and ducks, I do not know, but I do remember the Goat Lady coming. Occasionally, from the school bus, we would see, in the distance, across the fields, the Goat Lady with her herd of about forty goats. She was very tall and wore dark, flowing clothes and a tall witch-like hat. One day, after my father had left to join the army, she came in through our gate followed by some of the goats, while the rest were left in the road as there were so many of them. My mother went up to her with Nancy the goat. The Goat Lady turned and addressed the goats, "can this lady join our family", and then she walked off down the middle of the road followed by the goat herd plus one. Our goats were always tethered to trees, with chains, which frequently became tangled. The goats belonging to the Goat Lady were free and just followed her around. We also had a billy goat, which the Goat Lady did not want. One day, he escaped from a shed, and as my father had already joined the army, my mother asked a neighbour to help catch him. Years later, my mother told me that she spent much of her time running away from that neighbour, who was a bit of a womaniser. Eventually, Mr Harden (the farmer up the road) came and caught the goat, took him away and shot him.

During the war, Mr Harden shot one of our dogs, because it was a sheep chaser. He also shot one of our cats, called Spiteful, because it was too wild and could not be trusted with small children. At the beginning of the war, we were left with one pen of chickens, some rabbits and lots of empty sheds to play in.

I only spent one Christmas away from Oak Lodge as a child, and that was the first Christmas of the war when we went to the house of our grandmother in Folkstone. This was the house where my mother, her sister Vi and two brothers, Art and Billy were born and grew up. My Grandfather was permanently ill in hospital, so Auntie Vi and baby Michael lived with my grandmother as Uncle Manuel was away at sea, in the Royal Navy. It was a two bedroomed terraced house, and that Christmas, my grandmother slept in one bedroom, and we all slept in my aunt's bedroom. John and I topped and tailed in a single bed. Aunty Vi, my mother and Michael slept in the double bed, Valerie in Michael's cot and Lesley in Michael's pram downstairs. We woke up that Christmas day morning and at the bottom of the beds were very big colourful shop-bought Christmas stockings made of net, full of exciting things. I had a butcher's shop arrangement on a little wooden board and knife. The joints of meat and sausages were made of painted marshmallow tasting of dolly mixtures. I also had a tiny egg, which, when put into a glass of water, turned into a beautiful flower. I do not know how we travelled to Folkstone, or how we got home again, but I do remember falling down the stairs there and a wart on my knee disappearing.

I had one serious illness, bronchial pneumonia in the beginning of the second year of the war, and yellow jaundice towards the end of the war. According to my mother, I also caught chicken pox and whooping cough with scarlet fever, from my brother, in his first year at school, then measles in my second year at school. It was because I was recovering from measles and went outside in January to play in the snow, without a coat, that I got pneumonia; so my mother said. While I was ill in bed my mother sat in a low chair, by a little fire, while John slept in the other bed, in the back bedroom. My mother, who had been a nurse before she got married, made me a kaolin jacket of lint and Plaster of Paris. I picked the hard dried pieces off from around the edges. I was told that an army doctor came to the house and gave my mother some medication for me, probably sulphonamide, one of the first antibiotics. The shop, up the road, gave me a box of chocolates which were cut into quarters, to take with the medicine. Sweets were not rationed then, but very scarce. I must have been very ill because it left me with a bad heart, and a continuous cough, which drove my mother, trying for years, to find all sorts of remedies to cure me. A vinegar and sugar mixture, I liked, but some of the other cough mixtures like 'Liquifruiter' were horrible. As I had been so ill, it was Easter before I was allowed out of bed, and I was too frail to go to school, so spent the summer at home. Eventually, at the age of twenty one, in a London Hospital, I had an operation to remove the congested part of my lungs, so curing the cough.

In the year of 1940 I do not remember the war affecting my life very much. I can remember that summer my father coming home on leave and taking me on his bicycle to the village pub, to play with a boy called Peter Hawksworth who was in my class at school, and was the only son of the village publican. He had been very ill with Rheumatic Fever and was also too frail to go to school, so we played together the whole summer. At that time, a new pub was being built at the back of the old pub so we mainly played on the building site in the fine weather. Peter had some lovely toys, a whole room used for a train set layout and a playhouse like a big dog kennel. One day, we lit a fire in this house, and had to roll it over and over to put the fire out, before it set the whole site alight. Peter was a very pretty boy, with a mass of blond curls. His mother was beautiful too and wore lovely clothes and perfume. I always knew when she was near, as I could smell her perfume. Occasionally we would be taken by car to the house of a friend of hers. Once, I sat with Peter, on the edge of a bed, in a lovely bedroom, watching these two ladies in pretty silky lacy slips sitting in front of a dressing table. They were painting their fingers and toe nails bright red! They took a long time making up their faces. It was the first time I had seen mascara being used on eyelashes. They spent a long time doing each other's hair and they put on silk stockings which were kept up with suspenders. Sometimes we played with Ann, the daughter of the house; she was a bit older than us, and wore beautiful clothes, such as Shirley Temple dresses (as they were called in those days). That family also had another friend, who came to live along the road from us. My mother called her 'Ear-rings', and she also wore lovely clothes. All these ladies wore fur coats which I think my mother envied. My mother had very few clothes, and only wore stockings on special occasions, summer or winter. During the war her makeup was, Ponds Face Cream, Yardley's face powder, Max Factor lipstick, which she only wore to go out; which was not very often.

It was a lovely summer in 1940, and apart from my father going away, war was just an idea until on one particular day, a droning sound made us look up into the sky. In broad daylight, very high up in the sky, were blocks of planes flying in formation over our house, seeming to go on for ages. My mother said they were German planes, on their way to bomb London. Later that evening, she pointed to an orange glow in the sky, and said 'London's burning'. This was on 7th September 1940 and went down in history as 'The Blitz of London'.

Earlier that summer, we were fitted out with gas masks, grey and black for John, me and my mother, a red Mickey Mouse one for Valerie and for Lesley a great big one, to put the whole baby in, which hung around in the attic for years after the war. Later, an extra piece was attached to the gas masks which made them difficult to fit into the cases. We were told to carry them at all times. A distant cousin came to stay with us soon after the blitz, I do not remember her name, but she was an only child and was given John's bed in our room, one big drawer and one little drawer in the chest of drawers. The small drawer, she filled with money and sweets, which she never shared. She was allowed to go to the shop on her own to ring her parents from the phone box. She did not stay long because she was home sick and went back to her family.

I went back to school after the summer holidays, and was put back in the infants class, with all the new children, although I would be seven the following November. I thought to myself, I am not staying here. So I rapidly went through all the classes and eventually ended up sitting next to John, in the top class, and passed the eleven plus exam to go to Grammar school at the age of ten. Along one side of the infants' class room was a row of cupboards, and in one of these cupboards, on a shelf, were jars of 'Virol', and in each was a big spoon with a name-tape on the handle. I learned later that Virol was a food supplement containing vitamins given to children from poor families. Certain children would line up, and the child whose name was called, would stand in front of the teacher who popped a big spoonful of Virol into their mouths. They would lick the spoon clean, then wash it in the cloakroom sink, and give it back to the teacher, to put back in the cupboard. I loved Virol, and watched with envy, the children licking their spoons, but I was never put on the list. For Christmas that year, the teacher brought in some big walnut shells, we painted them gold and she helped us line the shells with material and tape two together, to make a case for a thimble, which she gave us to give our mothers for Christmas. My mother did not use a thimble but that thimble in its pretty container lived in her work basket for years. Also that Christmas, the classroom decks were pushed together to make a long table for a Christmas tea, for which my mother made some little pastry baskets filled with cherries and green jelly.

Auntie Georgie, a nursing friend of my mother's, came for Christmas that year.

During all the war years none of my father's family from London, ever came to visit us, but my father would regularly visit them when he was on leave. As my mother could not leave the children, he went on his own to my cousin Peggy's wedding in London. In a photograph we were given, the groom was wearing a kilt, which we children thought was very funny because we had never seen a man in a skirt before. My cousin, Beryl, was a bridesmaid in a long, frilly, pale green dress which I inherited, and for years it lived in the dressing up box. During the entire war, my mother's family and friends of our parents were our only visitors.

Sometime around the beginning of the war, the beaches were mined and covered in concrete blocks, iron spikes and barbed wire. Pill-Boxes were built at most cross roads, and every so often, anti-tank defences, a pile of big concrete blocks with iron spikes in, were placed at the edge of the road to block it, if necessary. We had great games climbing on the blocks, and went into the door-less Pill-Boxes, unless they were in a field of sheep, which made them mucky. Cows and horses were too big to get through the doorways. It seemed to me, that these strange buildings were part of the landscape and had always been there.

I still cannot picture the primary school, without the long brick built shelter, in the boys' playground. We had regular shelter practice, when the whole school trooped to the shelter in an orderly fashion, each class sitting on long forms against the walls, in allotted places. When the warning siren went off in the village, we all went to the shelter, and stayed there, until the all-clear siren went off. A most treasured possession, during the war, was a torch. Everywhere was so dark, particularly in the winter. There were no street lights in the towns or villages. We were used to having no street lights but we did miss the lights from the windows of houses. Windows had to be blacked-out; my mother was always checking the blackout curtains, as Wardens went round the houses after dark, looking for escaping light. We only had one sixty watt bulb in each room and learnt, from a very early age, that electricity was very expensive, so not to leave the light on when it was not needed. The winters were very cold during the war, and as there was no heating in the bedrooms, beautiful ice patterns formed on the inside of the windows. My mother would place little oil lamps, in particular places, to stop the water pipes freezing up and we did have stone hot water bottles wrapped in a cloth to put in the beds, which was very comforting. Sometimes these would fall out of the bed and land with a big thump on the lino floor in the middle of the night. My mother said that she could never find any rubber hot water bottles in the shops during the war.

I loved the snow, when the whole countryside became very quiet, as if a blanket had been laid over it, and cars crept slowly by on the road. John and I slid on ice-covered ponds and rolled huge snowballs across the fields. We would start with a small snowball and then roll it along the ground, picking up snow, until it became too big and heavy to move any further, then we would leave it there. Often, the snowballs we made in the fields would still be there when the rest of the snow had disappeared. I remember the day John and I put Lesley, in a new siren suit borrowed from Aunty Vi, on the edge of the pond to test the ice. She fell through and got soaked. We got a real telling off when we took her back to our mother, who stripped all her clothes off and gave her a hot bath. It seemed that we always had snow in the winter and for Christmas. Even now, I am disappointed when we have no snow in the winter.

Yet another change in our lives in the Spring of 1940, my grandmother, Auntie Vi and Michael moved to 'Wood View', a bungalow, five houses along the road from us. My grandmother had asked my mother if she could find somewhere for them to rent, because Folkestone was being shelled from France by the Germans and Auntie Vi was spending all day hiding under the kitchen table, with eighteen--month-old Michael. My mother knew Mr Edwards, who lived in the end bungalow, and luckily, someone had just moved out of one of the four bungalows he owned. So that summer, Nanna Beavis, Auntie Vi and Michael moved into a bungalow along the road from us and stayed for years. My grandmother died there at the age of ninety three. When they moved in, I can remember sitting on the grass, surrounded by stuffed toys; one was an enormous red and white rabbit with wired ears sticking up.

The following spring, Uncle Manuel, Auntie Vi's husband, came home on leave from the Navy and Michael became very upset with this strange man in his home. A two-year-old child, used to living with two women cannot be blamed for getting upset, when a man, who had been away for a year, suddenly comes back into his life. As a result, my uncle spent most of his time at our house, which pleased me, as I enjoyed his company. This was the last time we saw Uncle Manuel, as later that year, he was reported missing at sea. He never saw his second son, Robin, who was born the following January 1942. The loss of the cruiser HMS Neptune, sunk off the Italian coast, was one of the least known World War 2 naval disasters. Over 800 lives were lost and there was just a single survivor. This left my mother, my aunt and my grandmother to look after six children. My father came home on leave occasionally and Uncle Art came home on leave, from the Merchant Navy, to my grandmother's house. He was her eldest son and not yet married. Uncle Billy, my mother's younger brother, had also been in the Merchant Navy, but had married in Australia before the war and stayed there.

Mummy, Lesley, John, Avril, Valerie, Rags and Kitty Wee

Daddy and Mummy 1940

John, Binkie, Michael, Lesley, Valerie and Avril.
Wartime on the Farm.

Avril, Nanna Beavis, John,
Valerie and Michael. 1938.

1939 Daddy
John, Mummy, Avril
Valerie and Lesley

29

Chapter 3

I was very proud of my father being a soldier and always looked forward to his coming home on leave. I helped him plant the potatoes in the spring and dig them up in the autumn. These were left to dry on sacks, then sorted and stored in a bunker in the Iron Shed. He planted runner beans which ran up bean poles that our father coppiced from the hazelnut trees in the wood. He planted lots of cabbages which became infested with the caterpillars of cabbage: white butterflies.

John and I were given jam jars with string handles, half full of paraffin, and our job was to pick the caterpillars off the cabbage leaves and put them in the jars to die. This was a never ending job as my childhood summer days were filled with butterflies and moths. In the spring, tiny loop the loop caterpillars on fine sink

Fly Paper

threads would get on my clothes and in my hair when going down the paths in the wood. Maybe it was because I lived in the country; there seem to be many more insects about as, on hot summer days, bees could be heard buzzing about and flies were everywhere. Our mother hung fly papers in the kitchen and these would be covered in flies in no time at all. Fly papers were a small cardboard tube containing a roll of paper which, when pulled out, made a very sticky ringlet that hung from the ceiling. These were usually placed above the table to prevent hair accidentally getting caught in them and when thrown on the fire, went up in a sheet of flame with a sizzling sound. Tomatoes and cucumbers were planted in the greenhouse built on the side of the house and when our father went away again, we helped my mother to look after the vegetable garden. During his limited time at home, our father tried to produce enough logs to last the winter, which meant manually chopping down trees and sawing them into logs. Occasionally our mother would have to buy extra logs from Mr Harden who delivered them by tractor with a trailer that tipped up and dumped the load just inside the front gate. John and I would be enlisted to move and stack the logs into the garage near the house to keep them dry.

The only fire lit every day, in the winter, was in the living room. Each day the ashes from the fireplace were cleared, and a new fire was laid. First, screwed up newspaper was laid in the grate, then sticks made from chopped up planks from the workshop, and finally a few lumps of coal; the paper was then lit and fanned to get the fire started. When it was well alight, logs were laid on it for the rest of the day and maybe a few lumps of coal. This meant a great deal of precious coal and log carrying and I can remember my mother in the evening, putting the sticks to dry by the fire, to light it the next day.

Each year our father would move the chicken house and fence off a new run for the twelve to twenty laying hens and one cockerel, (plus the few extra until Christmas). Near the house, each spring, a couple of broody hens were put in nesting broody cages to sit on 13 eggs each. These cages had slatted fronts so the hen could be seen sitting on the nest. Every day our mother let the hens out to be fed and watered; often she would have to lift the hens off their nests because they were reluctant to leave the eggs. After the chicks hatched, they wandered around the garden near the house with the mother hen, until they became such a nuisance and were put in the chicken run with the other chickens. The female chicks were kept to replace the laying hens but the males were only kept until Christmas when they became dinners for the family.

Even though I was the eldest girl in the family, I did very little housework, but John and I did help with some of the outside jobs, and one of these was to shut the chickens up at night. The chicken house was situated near the wood, which was quite a distance from the house, and the chickens would only go inside as it got dark. This meant, in the winter, when we got home from school, John and I would go together to shut the door of the chicken house to stop the foxes getting in and killing them. It would always be a race to get back to the house first, he nearly always won. For years I would have a particular nightmare about a tiger running out of the wood and chasing me back to the house. I found it extremely difficult to run in the nightmare.

At the beginning of the war everybody was given an identity card and a ration book.

DJGH94 was my identity card number. For me, the only news of the war came from my mother who listened to the news on the wireless and read the Daily Express, and, of course, from my brother who was obsessed with anything to do with war. The wireless (as we called it), sat on a shelf in the corner of the living room and sometimes we listened to Uncle Mac on Children's Hour. The newspaper was delivered daily and our mother did the crossword each day, as well as the skeleton crossword on Sundays which sometimes took her the whole week to finish. As children, we looked forward to each day, to the adventures of Rupert Bear and one of us would get a Rupert Bear Annual for Christmas.

Our mother, who was always there, was the centre of our lives and entirely on her own, had to manage the household on a soldier's pay which she received through an allowance book at the Post Office. Tradesmen still delivered and had to be paid in coupons, together with the money. In the beginning, some food was rationed, but as the war continued, more and more items became rationed, such as clothes and household linen. Many things were in short supply and on one occasion, our mother tried to obtain permits to buy some rubber boots for us; she did not succeed because we lived on a main road. Once the ditch in front of our house overflowed across the drive; having no rubber boots, and the water being too deep for us to walk across, the driver, in his rubber boots, got out of the bus and carried us across. She did manage to get a permit for a box of water colour paints, which were very precious and not to be wasted. We always had a good supply of paper and pencils, which our father brought with him, when he came home on leave. We did not have coloured pencils, but we did have coloured chalks.

When I was well enough to go back to school after the summer holidays, Auntie Vi made me a very posh blue and white striped canvas bag with handles for my lunch tin and a matching one for my gas mask. I stayed in the infants' class until Christmas then went up into the middle class. It was during my time in the middle class that children evacuated from London were billeted in the village and the surrounding area. As so many of them were of primary school age and Hamstreet School could not accommodate them all; it was decided that the local children would be taught in the morning and the evacuees in the afternoon. Most of these evacuee children were billeted with families in the village and I do not remember meeting any of them. The London children did not stay in our area very long and were relocated somewhere much safer.

During that summer term I had more time off school because John and I caught impetigo. As it was mainly in our noses, our faces were painted blue with Gentian Violet. I remember that at the same time, there was an outbreak of nits in the school. Our mother blamed the evacuees and would inspect our heads daily. All the time I was at school, a nurse would come regularly to inspect everyone's heads for nits. This was very annoying because I had to undo my plaits and could not do those up again, as my mother always plaited my hair.

Because my mother's habit of putting Iodine on cuts and bruises was very painful, we tried not to tell her when we were injured. Sometimes the secret wounds went septic, which meant the poultice treatment. A piece of lint wrapped in a cloth was put in boiling water then wrung out to remove most of the water. The still very hot lint was placed on the wound, repeated two or three times, then iodine was applied before bandaging with strips of old sheet. My mother told me that while she was a nurse on night duty, one of the tasks was to roll up bandages made of old sheets. Because the local children had missed so much schooling, Mr. Ainsworth, the headmaster decided to open the school in the summer holidays by himself. John and I attended, and as there was no school bus, we walked the two miles there and back. I really enjoyed this time and for some reason ordinary lessons were not allowed to be taught, so we played games, spent time drawing and painting, playing with plasticine, reading books and having books read to us. Boys and girls were allowed to play anywhere in the school grounds together, so I went to places in the school that were normally out of bounds. The school closed halfway through the holiday, however, because not enough children were attending, so it was back home again for us, to run wild in the fields and woods.

For the first year of the war, our mother found it a struggle on her own but when, in the second year of the war, Auntie Vi, Michael and Nanna Beavis moved into Wood View, life became a lot easier for her. My grandmother had been a cook in a big house, and had remained unmarried until she was thirty years old. This was because her future husband had to look after his widowed mother until she died. Our Grandmother had four children, one every two years, before our grandfather joined the army at the beginning of World War 1 and was sent to India. He became ill after the war and ended his days in the Chartham Asylum. Ever so often our grandmother would visit him, but would never allow anybody else to go with her. I never knew him, but at some time during the Second World War, he died and I went to his funeral at Orlestone Church. I was told that he fell out of bed, broke his hip and died of pneumonia. I later learned that he had been wounded in World War 1 and the lead in the shrapnel left in his body after surgery eventually drove him insane. There was a large picture of our grandfather on the wall, in our grandmother's house, to which I could see a likeness to my brother.

When Auntie Vi first came to Wood View, she was married with one small boy, within a year she was widowed, with two small boys to bring up on her own. Not long after moving there, on one particular day, we were having our dinner sitting around the kitchen table, when Auntie Vi came in with Michael (at that time they called him Mimey). While she was talking to our mother, Michael crawled under the kitchen table and tried to bite our legs, so we kicked him and he cried so we said he had banged his head. He was very spoilt and we did not like him very much, but he always wanted to come to our house to play. We put up with the excuses for his bad behaviour from my aunt, who said he was lacking, in what? We never knew. The day came when he bit his baby brother, Robin. My aunt brought him along the road, threw him in through our mothers kitchen door, telling her that she could have him, as he was such a spiteful child. She then shut the door and went back home. This was not much of a punishment as Michael liked being at Oak Lodge.

I have realised, the older one gets, the quicker time flies by, so for me, as a child growing up in the war years, time went by very slowly. The winters were very severe and we always had snow. All the floors in our house were covered in linoleum which our mother mopped every day and polished occasionally, this made the long passage down the centre of the house a great slide. The house was very draughty and in winter, the only warm places were in front of the living room fire and in the kitchen. When we came home from school, the oven was on, more often than not, and the dinner was cooking. As the evening wore on, the living room, with the door shut, became warmer but the kitchen became colder and colder and we still had to wash at the kitchen sink with water heated in the electric kettle. We had just one sink with a cold water tap. All the hot water in the house had to be heated in the electric kettle, or in saucepans on the stove. We cleaned our teeth at the kitchen sink, rubbing our tooth brushes on a solid tablet of pink toothpaste in a round metal tin, everybody used the same toothpaste but at least we all had our own tooth brushes.

In the very cold weather, our mother would put a paraffin stove in the hallway at night, which would be moved into the kitchen in the morning while we were getting ready for school. When it was cold, I slept in a large brass ended double bed, with my two little sisters and a china hot water bottle wrapped up in a blanket. In the winter, the indoor lavatory always had a little lit paraffin lamp in it, which sometimes made it the warmest room in the house. We were privileged to have an indoor toilet, as most houses only had outdoor toilets, often down a long garden path. 'Going to the toilet' has replaced 'Going to the lav', the term we used then. The very shiny and semi-transparent toilet paper was called Bronco, was not very practical, but was very useful for tracing.

In the winter, on school mornings, I got up and dressed in the cold, then went down the two steps to the nice warm kitchen. I cannot remember what I had for breakfast, or the contents of my lunch tin. My mother would plait my hair, find my glasses and make sure we were all ready for school with our lunch boxes and gas masks, to be picked up by 'The Tub'. The school bus, like all cars and buses at the time, was cold, because there was no heating. At school, there was no heating in the cloakrooms. The toilet block was down a long path and open to the elements. The classrooms were not particularly warm, as each was only heated by a big coke stove situated by the teacher's desk. It was so draughty, with high windows all round, and high ceilings, making it very cold sitting at a desk at the back of room. The sandwiches I had for lunch were cold and sometimes the bottle of milk I had in the morning break was frozen, pushing the little cardboard cap out on a stalk of frozen cream. Every winter I got chilblains on my fingers but mainly on my toes, which swelled up, itched and sometimes burst. They then got the poultice, iodine and sheet bandage treatment. It did not help that the leather shoes I wore were not very good at keeping feet dry. Every evening our mother would polish everybody's shoes and put them in front of the fire to dry, ready for the morning. My brother was always asking our mother to buy him boots with studs, so he could slide in the playground and make sparks fly. She would never allow him to have boots, but our father did put some segs on his shoes. These were little kidney shaped metal studs put on the heels and soles of shoes to protect the leather. Heels and soles of leather shoes were always wearing out, so either my father would mend them at home or they would be taken to the shoe mender in the village.

One winter, the boys made a long ice slide in their sloping playground, which looked a lot of fun, but, unfortunately, girls were not allowed to play there. Even in the coldest weather, John and I would go out to play, particularly if there was snow and ice about. When it snowed, the countryside became very quiet, just the crunching sound of shoes on snow and when walking through the woods, an occasional fall of snow from the trees would spook us. We would follow animal tracks in the snow and clear the paths to the chickens, the rabbits, the log shed, the coal bunker and the front gate. When we were at school, our mother would have to clear the snow on her own. I can still remember how painful it was; warming up freezing cold hands and feet. To this day, I try not to let my hands and feet get too cold, to avoid the agony. In those days, I was so glad I had a mother, an aunt and grandmother to knit me jumpers, socks and gloves. Because all of our clothes were made of natural materials, they wore out quickly, so our mother was continually mending them and darning socks and gloves.

Before the war, we would often see a family visiting Mrs Wilson, next door. Mr Weeks, the father, was an old man with a long beard, in a wheelchair, pushed by Mrs Weeks with two small girls, Doreen and Edwina, on either side. They lived round the corner in Shadoxhurst Road and the children came to our school. In their lunch boxes they had tiny, three cornered, butter and mustard sandwiches wrapped in a cotton table napkin. Oddly, I have no clear recollection of the contents of my own lunch tin. The girls were very old fashioned and wore dresses down to their ankles. When their father died at the beginning of the war, Mrs Weeks moved into Mrs Wilson's house next door and the girls went to a Masonic boarding school and only came home for holidays. When Mrs Wilson's husband died, not long after the start of the war, she went to work in London.

Then, to our mother's dismay, a Rag and Bone family, together with their horse and cart, moved into the house on the other side of us. The 'Foster family' consisted of a tiny, thin little mother with a cleft palette, which made her very difficult to understand, and six children, Doris; Olive; Ronnie; Dorothy; Ernie and Freddy, and two rather sinister looking uncles that ran the Rag and Bone business. My mother told me that the business had belonged to the children's father, but he had been killed and all the children had money put in trust for them when they reached a certain age. The children were very thin, pale and very poorly dressed. They wore shoes with no socks, even in the winter. They never came out to play with us; I just saw them on the bus and at school. One day I went behind the garage and through the hedge; I could see into their scullery because the door was open. The children were sitting side by side on a long form, each eating a baked potato in their hands. When one of the uncles asked our mother if he could have access and fence off part of our land to put the horse in, she agreed as long as it was used solely for that purpose. The front of their house was covered in huge piles of clothes; bedsteads; rusting iron; cans; bottles; a couple of carts and an old car. It was a typical rag and bone yard. They did only use the land and a shed for the horse, but one day it got out and came down the path to our house. Our mother did not like horses at all, stayed inside, and sent my brother round to the neighbours to let them know. One day, a very old fluffy white rabbit of ours went missing. Our mother must have suspected something because she called the police. The policeman came to our house and in our living room, while we were watching, questioned the older children about what they had eaten for dinner. They were very quiet and said nothing. The rabbit skin was found next door and not long after that, the family moved round the corner to Bromley Green Road. Our mother did say that the rabbit had not been eaten by us because it was too old and must have been very tough. Another family moved in next door, a granny, a mother, and a little boy called Teddy Reeves.

Nanna Beavis, Auntie Vi, Michael, Robin
and Monty.

Chapter 4

The Iron Shed

As I grew older and the war continued, life for me became more interesting. Valerie started school and our mother went to work as a nurse at the Grosvenor Hospital in Ashford. As nurseries or places to leave children under five did not exist in those days, Lesley was left with Auntie Vi who was at home caring for Michael and Robin. One day our mother come home from work and said how amazed she had been when a German plane flew by, very low, on the level with the balcony she was working on with T.B. patients, and the pilot waved to them. She gave up nursing when Jacky was born and Auntie Vi then went to work on the farm. At the beginning of the war, we were the only house in our road to have an Anderson Shelter delivered. This type of shelter had to be built half above and half below the ground. We lived opposite a big pond, so the water table was quite high, so every time the hole was dug, it filled with water. In our drive, this unused shelter remained a decaying, rusting heap of metal, on which I remember cutting my wrist. This wound went septic, and once again I received the usual poultice and iodine treatment.

Planes would fly over, some high, some very low, and occasionally there would be a dog fight. John and I enjoyed watching these, but, when we were at home, our mother would shout for us to go indoors, particularly when bullet casings could be heard pinging on the roof of the house. Sometimes we would see a plane shot down, and get on our bicycles to try and reach the plume of black smoke. Very often, we would cycle for ages and never reach it. John had his own bike, but I would have to ride my mother's bike, by standing up on the pedals, as the seat was too high for me. On one occasion, a bomber came down in Shadoxhurst, which was quite close, so off we went on our bikes. I saw the smoking plane wreckage, though the trees behind the Public house, and a man on a parachute hanging in a tree. Then a Warden suddenly appeared shouting, "Unexploded bombs on board", so we turned round and raced back home. I did not hear any explosions so I am not sure he was telling the truth. It was difficult to approach the site of a plane that had just been shot down, because the military appeared very quickly to keep the public away. Later, I would visit these sites with John, as he searched the area for bits of planes for his collection. One memorable day, at the site of a crashed plane, I found, against a fence, a bloody boot with a lot of flies buzzing around and what looked like a sock and a foot in it!

For the first couple of years, an occasional army convoy would trundle by the house; a jeep at the front with a green flag and the last vehicle in the convoy had a red flag.

Sometimes, a convoy of tanks would go by; the noise they made could be heard long before they arrived and long after they had gone. The marks the tank tracks made in the road stayed for ages. When I got up for school one morning, the living room was full of sleeping soldiers. Outside, there was a tank in the drive, and army vehicles all along the edge of the road.

Soldiers were also sleeping on the hay that was kept for the rabbits, in the iron shed. It was a school day, so as usual, we got ready and caught 'The Tub', and when we got home from school, they had all gone. Our mother gave them a portable gramophone and some records which we did not miss, because we had another in a cabinet, which we could wind up and play. The gramophone needles were never replaced during the war, so the quality of the sound was very poor. We did not have any new records until some years after the war. At the beginning of the war, when our grandparents moved to a smaller house in Eltham, (as their house in Hackney had been bombed), a van load of furniture came our way, including a piano. My mother played the piano and we sung along. She also played a zither and banjo, which, I believed, belonged to her brothers. We had one dog that would howl when we had a singing session. It was during the war that my grandfather died and a trunk full of his clothes was sent for our father to wear. These proved unsuitable for our father who was a lot taller and thinner than his father, so our mother gave the Homburg hats, pin striped trousers and black jackets to the gypsies, but kept the white shirts to recycle. The thought of the gypsies wearing my Grandfather's clothes would make her smile. The trunk also contained a fox fur which hung on our hall stand for many years. This was real fox skin, including the head with glass eyes that was worn round the neck and fastened with a big clip that was shaped like a fox's mouth. A wooden box of Goss china came with the trunk. There was a golf ball, a cricket bag and all sorts of small shapes in white china, each with the name of a town and a heraldic shield on it. Our mother did not like them at all, so we were given them to play with, but we did not find them very useful. After my grandfather died, I remember my mother saying that certain items, such as a bookcase and side board, had our father's name written on the underside of the drawers by his own father.

I did not have many clothes, one set on, one set in the wash, one set in the drawer and maybe one set for best. One chest of drawers was big enough to hold all the children's clothes, one drawer each. Our parents had the only wardrobe and dressing table in their bedroom which held all their clothes. Another chest of drawers held all the household linen. The one dressing gown belonging to my father hung on the back of their bedroom door for years. Clothes had to be hand washed, dried, ironed and aired. This was a real problem in the winter and on rainy days, as they had to be dried in front of the one and only fire in the living room, or on a line in the kitchen. When our mother hung clothes outside, in the very cold weather, they would freeze on the line, become as stiff as a board and stand up on their own. Very often, they would freeze dry. There were no washing machines, spin dryers or tumble dryers and clothes that were mangled, retained a lot of water which meant they took a long time to dry. All my childhood, the nearest clothing shops to us were in Ashford and these were open from nine in the morning to five thirty in the evening, Monday to Friday, and on Saturday from nine to one thirty. The rest of the time, the windows were shuttered, so window shopping could only be done in daylight hours. In the winter, the shutters came down as soon as it got dark. All the clothes were behind the counter and one day I went with my mother to buy a blouse for her. We waited in a queue to be served, then when we finally got to the counter; my mother gave her size to the shop assistant who took three packets from the shelves behind the counter. She carefully took out the blouses out of the cellophane packets and laid them one by one on the counter for my mother to look at. When my mother asked the assistant if she had any others, she said, "Sorry, that's it".

Marks and Spencer's then, only sold clothes, and was the only place where clothes were laid on the counter to be looked at. Woolworths was the only other shop where one could look at goods laid out on counters, but they did not sell clothes. Most household linen was in short supply and had to be ordered; it was very expensive and used up a lot of precious clothing coupons. I can remembering my mother turning sheets, sides to middle, which meant, cutting the sheet in half and sewing the not so worn edges together. When these wore out, the best bits were used to make pillow cases and tea towels; the rest was turned into polishing rags, dish cloths and bandages.

The ladies in our family belonged to the Women's Institute and our grandmother regularly went to church. Once or twice a year, a bazaar was held in the village hall to raise money for the church. Different stalls were arranged around the room and always in one corner was a rummage stall, run by my grandmother and Auntie Vi. This stall was made up of piles old clothes donated by local people, and as my relations ran this stall, they had first pick. I can remember helping them set up this stall, hanging some clothes on a rail and heaping the rest on trestle tables. I also helped with the teas. When the rummage stall was opened, there was a lot of pushing and clothes flying all over the place. Most of the clothes were sold for a few pence, and my mother was always very pleased with these second-hand clothes as she and Auntie Vi recycled most of them to make clothes for us girls. I had a very pretty dress made from a jumble sale dress and a lovely swimming costume. I remember unpicking knitted garments for the wool but sometimes moth holes would make it very difficult to get a decent length of wool to knit with. My first shop bought woolly was a school sweater when I started Grammar School. I also had shop bought square neck blouses; gym slip; raincoat; a beret with a red tassel; indoor and outdoor shoes; plimsolls; a school scarf; a school blazer; a satchel and navy blue knickers that cost five shillings a pair. The gym slip was washed only during the holidays and half term because the box pleats had to be tacked down before washing drying and pressing. My mother and aunt made all our summer dresses, some with knickers to match. The elastic used in these knickers was taken out every time they were washed, and put back in and fastened with a safety pin. A whole bunch of these knicker elastics on safety pins, hung on a hook on the dresser. One day, a huge battered cardboard box full of the most beautiful children's' clothes arrived. These fitted Lesley and were passed on to Jacky. The parcel came from an army friend of my father, whose little girl had died. There were coats, beautiful smocked dresses and among the clothes was a little pleated dress that had to be tacked before washing and pressing; needless to say, it was only worn on special occasions.

It was lovely in the winter to come home from school to the lovely warm kitchen, with our mother cooking dinner and the fire alight in the living room. We always ate our meals in the kitchen and sat in the same places round the table. Our mother sat near the stove, next to her was the high chair, usually with a baby in it, then me. John sat on the other side of our mother in our father's armchair, unless our father was home; then we all moved round. As the girls grew older and were replaced by a younger child in the high chair, they were put in places between John and me. As the war years went by, the china plates and cups got broken and could not be replaced, so for everyday use, we ended up with enamel plates and mugs; the best china was kept for special occasions. My mother loved china and, today, would have been in her element buying up all the tea sets in the charity shops. We always had a dog, often patiently sitting by the high chair, waiting for food to drop. The high chair was also used when my mother cut the boys' hair. In the summer holidays, the table and chairs were put outside in the garden, and we had most of meals there. It never seemed to rain during that time.

In the winter, when the weather was too bad to go out and play, we had to amuse ourselves, so occasionally, our mother would allow us to turn the sitting room upside down to play the game of getting round the room without touching the floor. We had a bookshelf in the hall that was full of books, mostly boring, belonging to our father. Among these were two big art books of black and white, and a few coloured pictures of world famous paintings. I loved these books, but it was a great surprise to me when I did eventually see some of these paintings for real, that some were really enormous and filled a whole wall while others were quite small. As the paintings were all the same size in the book, I assumed they would all be about the size of the pictures I had seen on the walls of rooms in houses. My particular favourite book in the bookcase was 'The Blue Bird' a school prize of my mother's; it became so worn that some years later, my father accidentally burned it together with other stuff from the attic. For years I tried to find a copy of this book to give to my mother, but she died before I managed to trace a copy in Canada using the internet.

My mother would get me books from the library. There were not many children's books in the library, just two shelves in one corner. I loved reading and my mother would say, "She's always got her nose in a book" and sometimes she would tell me off for reading in the daytime. Access to books was very limited during the war, but Auntie Vi, before the war, had belonged to a book club, so on the book shelves at our grandmother's house, there were many of the classics: Shakespeare, Dickens, the Brontes, the complete works of Bernard Shaw and many others. These, I would sneak along the road to read or borrow. Our mother was a great reader and would often read to us; she knew a great many poems and would recite lines from Shakespeare. Every week, she and Auntie Vi went to the library to get books for themselves and me. Children were allowed one book each and adults three. On very rare occasions, when I went shopping with my mother, we would go to the library and I could choose my own book from the very limited selection on two low down shelves. One day I chose 'The Blue Book of Fairy Tales' ,which I loved, and when I found out there was a whole series of these books, in all the colours of the rainbow, my mother would try and get one whenever she went to the library. The Stanley Gibbons Stamp Catalogue was the one book John asked my mother to get him from the library. In those days, stamps from the whole world were in one book. He was very proud of his stamp album and spent hours studying stamps and spent some of his hard earned money on packets of stamps. Years later, as I rearranged a stamp collection of many volumes, inherited by my grandson, I thought how much my brother would have enjoyed a collection like that in the war years. My brother seldom read storybooks but was an avid reader of comics and newspapers and anything to do with war. His main interest was planes and he collected cards with black and white silhouettes of English and foreign planes. He used these to identify the planes flying above us. He was very seldom wrong when he got me to test him using these cards. He joined the Air force when he was sixteen and served for many years.

There were no toy shops in Ashford during the war, but there was one shop called 'Geerings', that sold books. Every time my mother went to Ashford, she would go to this shop to look at the books and sometimes order some for our birthdays and Christmas. 'The Flower Fairy' books, and the books by Enid Blyton that she bought, were particularly enjoyed. 'The Enchanted Wood' series of books were the absolute favourites and reading them over and over again to my sisters; my children; my grandchildren and now my great grandchildren, has given me great pleasure. For many years, Enid Blyton books were considered unsuitable for children, and were unavailable in libraries and schools. After many years, these books were on sale again, with chapters missing and many of the names changed, but still my great grandchildren love these stories.

Plasticine must have been available during the war because we played with it at school and it was one of our favourite materials to play with at home. One year, for our birthdays, John and I both wanted plasticine. During the war, we had one present only for birthdays. John, of course, had his present on his birthday, a big box of plasticine in ten rolls of beautiful colours; I had to wait eleven days for mine. However much we tried to keep the colours separate, all the plasticine always ended up the same khaki colour. This colour was perfect for John, who spent hours modelling tiny armies of lorries, jeeps, tanks and planes.

We would then have a war using the beads as bombs and anything the beads hit had to be crushed, so all ended up in the same khaki plasticine ball, ready to make another army. We had a few old puzzles with pieces missing. There were two 250 piece puzzles of cottage paintings that John and I would have a race to see who could finish first. The Snow White and Seven Dwarf puzzle had lots of pieces missing, and the 2000 piece Daily Express Advert puzzle took a long time to finish and was kept under the table cloth for days. These were the only puzzles we had during the war. We had a cribbage board which belonged to our father, who taught John and I to play, and it was the only game I played with our mother. There was an old bagatelle board that had lost its steel ball, but we discovered it worked just as well with marbles. We also had a dart board and some moth eaten darts. We had to be very careful when we played darts, because of the smaller children, but I do remember John and I were playing one day, when a dart he threw bounced off the board, went through my shoe and into my little toe. That toe had the poultice and iodine treatment straight away, did not get septic, and healed nicely.

John and I were the only children in our family to remember the wonderful Christmases before the war. My sisters and cousins had only wartime childhood Christmas memories which were very basic, and this carried on for some years after the war. So our mother, John and I (with very limited resources), made Christmas for the little ones. We always had a big Christmas tree, which John and I would go into the forest and choose during the day, returning after dark, to cut it down and drag it home across the fields. This was decorated with the lights and baubles, but as the war went on, the lights failed to work and the baubles gradually got broken and could not be replaced. One year, our mother bought some coloured cellophane; red; green; yellow; and purple, which we used to wrap two or three sweets in little bundle to tie on the Christmas tree. It looked very effective. Every year, our mother saved our sweet ration from October to December, so we could have special sweets for Christmas, usually a tin of Quality Street. Always available every Christmas, were packs of strips of coloured paper, to make paper chains which were stuck together with flour paste, which our mother made, and these were hung across the ceiling. Very often, when it was damp or there was steam about, the paper chains would come unstuck and fall down. The flour paste was also used for hanging wall paper. John and I knew where to find the best holly and ivy in the fields and woods to put in vases and decorate the mirrors and pictures.

On Christmas Eve, John and I helped our mother decorate the house and tree after the little girls had gone to bed and put my father's old socks at the end of the beds. We filled the socks with an orange, some nuts and sweets, and wrapped the girls' presents. For Christmas we always had parcels from the relations in London. The presents for John and I were wrapped by our mother, then she put all the presents at the bottom of our beds after we were asleep. When I woke up on Christmas morning, I would stretch my feet down to the bottom of the bed and feel the rustling paper. I always had a new book to read. One year, our mother and Auntie Vi made two rag dolls called, Raggedy Ann and Andy, for

Valerie and Lesley. While we were all in one bed playing with the presents, our mother was lighting the fires in the living room and front room, preparing the food for the day. I always looked forward to, and really enjoyed, Christmas dinner in the middle of the day. We always had one of our own chickens with stuffing; roast potatoes; Yorkshire pudding (a big one in a pie dish); carrots; tinned peas [frozen peas were not invented]; sprouts followed by Christmas pudding with custard. Our mother was a good cook, and everything was made from basic ingredients, as readymade food was not available. Silver three penny pieces were put in the pudding and we were delighted when we found one, but these had to be given back, and were kept in a wooden pot, on the mantel piece for the following year. After Christmas dinner, we were allowed to go in the front room and play until tea time. My grandmother, Auntie Vi, Michael and Robin came along in the afternoon and stayed for tea. The boys had extra presents from the children of war widows' fund. One year, Michael received a Meccano set, which he was a bit too young for, so John helped him build things, and so we all had good games with these toys. I always enjoyed Christmas tea: we had tinned ham sandwiches; tin salmon sandwiches; cheese straws; sausage rolls; chocolate biscuits; mince pies; jelly; a rabbit blancmange; tinned fruit salad with evaporated milk and Christmas cake. One year, Michael had a temper because he wanted to eat only chocolate biscuits, and our mother allowed him only two. Our Grandmother got annoyed, and said as it was Christmas; he should be able to eat whatever he liked. Once a year, at Christmas, one packet of chocolate biscuits was allocated to each house, and Michael had already eaten the packet allocated to their house. The only drinks I can remember at Christmas are one bottle of port; one bottle of sherry and some bottles of fizzy drinks (which I did not like). During all those years, Christmas Day was the only day I can remember having supper and a drink before going to bed.

Paper Chains

Paper Bell from 'The Neptune'

Quality Street Sweets in Celephane Wraps.

Holly.

Chapter 5

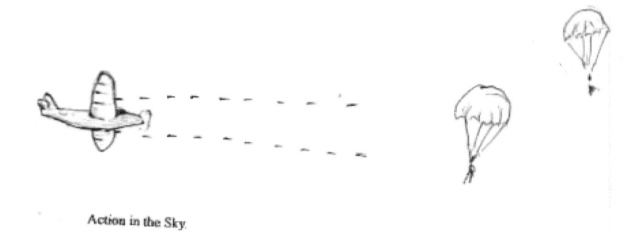

Action in the Sky

Oak Lodge was a great natural playground, but as my brother and I grew older, we explored more and more of the surrounding countryside. All the woods and fields, in every direction, gradually became as familiar to us as our own property, and we were never told off for trespassing. On the other side of the road, opposite Oak Lodge, was a five bar gate leading into a field with a large pond in a small wood. We children spent many happy hours playing on this gate, swinging on it, vaulting over it, or just sitting on it. We never left the gate open, because this field led to other fields that had cows or sheep in them. All the time I lived at Oak Lodge, an old black horse called Bess lived in these fields, and often came to the gate for us to give her bread. Sometime during the war, pylons (thick ropes slung between tall metal poles) were put across some large fields, to stop gliders landing. After the war, we collected some of this rope to make swings, and in our wood, we made our own assault course between two oak trees. About the same time, all through the woods and fields, we found strips of silver foil, dropped by planes, which we collected to make Christmas decorations.

Across the field, in front of the house was 'The Forest', as we called it. Years later, I found out that it really was a forest. Originally it had been deciduous woodland, but at some time before the war, part of it was felled to make charcoal. We found the remains of the iron rings of the charcoal burners, rusting in the undergrowth. The occasional oak tree had been left and the rest of the area was planted with small fir trees. During the war, because the trees were so small, the area was very open, but, by the end of the war, these trees had grown to the height of about two meters. In the summer, it was very hot walking down the heather lined lanes (fire breaks), compared with the cool of the woods, and always in the summer, the hum of insects; grasshoppers; bees; lots of butterflies; moths; mosquitoes and lizards. John and I tried to catch these lizards, but very often we were left with a wriggling tail between our fingers as they ran away. Sometimes, John caught a slow worm to take home and let go in our wood, but I did not like the feel of them, so did not touch them. Sometimes we would see a snake, but we never tried to catch one. In the years after the war, my father collected all the grass cuttings in a heap and covered them with corrugated iron sheets. When he lifted a sheet up, there was nearly always a snake or two underneath, much to the delight of the grandchildren. In the part of the forest that had been left as natural woodland, was a pond; we would visit in the spring, to look for Moorhens' eggs. We would often see snakes swimming in it, so we called it 'The Snake Pond'. In summer, we picked water lilies there, by quickly running over the floating moss before it sank under our weight. After the war, the pine trees grew very thick and tall, so nothing much grew under them. But in the sunny drives we picked primroses, wild strawberries and gathered bunches of heather, which was the only place it grew in all the woods that we were aware of.

As there were very few houses in the area, the RAF used it to attempt to shoot down enemy aircraft. There was the occasional dog fight, but not many planes shot down. This altered dramatically when the Doodlebugs appeared in June 1944. These flew on regular flight paths, one over our house, and one to the right and another to the left. They did not come at regular times, but always on the same flight path. Many were shot down over the Channel, but the ones that got through had to be shot down before reaching London, which made the area we were living in, very dangerous. The forest was also the place where planes dropped their spare fuel tanks. These were fuel-filled, large, egg shaped containers, made of thick cardboard; carried under the wings of a plane. This allowed the plane to refuel and stay up in the sky longer. Most of the time, they disintegrated when they hit the ground but occasionally we would find one that had survived the impact. We would turn it into a small boat by cutting the top off and putting a board across the middle to sit on, and, using a plank of wood as an oar, we would row across ponds. It floated, but was not very stable, and would gradually become water logged and sink. But we had some fun with it. In the forest, there were no ditches or dykes, just ponds.

Our wood and the woods belonging to other people, at the back of our house, were full of ditches and dykes, and very damp. Our father constantly dug and cleared ditches, to make sure the water was always flowing. The water flowed through ditches that criss-crossed along the edges of the paths, and through the grounds, of Oak Lodge, ending up in the big ditch at the end of the field, at the back of our wood. We were always falling in these ditches and getting wet feet. These ditches fed into bigger ditches called dykes that went through the surrounding woods and fields. John and I went bird nesting in these woods, following the dykes, and crossing them on makeshift bridges, some just a single blank. In one place somebody had made a bridge from an old car frame that was quite tricky to crawl across. One year, when John was negotiating this iron frame, his pen knife must have fallen out of his pocket. We recovered it the following spring, having spotted it shining in the water under the bridge. In other places, most of the bridges were made of big heavy wooden planks. One year, we decided we could do with a couple of these planks, so we dismantled a bridge; put the planks in the water and floated them down the dykes and ditches to the back of our wood and put them in an empty shed. Some years later, when our father made a see-saw for us all, he did not question where the big plank had come from. On one occasion, we put the see-saw plank up against the shed roof to make a slide and I remember Michael sliding down it and getting such a big splinter in his bottom that he was taken to the hospital to have it cut out. The woods adjoining our wood were only useful for bird nesting; picking bluebells; wood anemones and orchids, (which our mother said, smelts like tom cats). Primroses did not grow there.

Barton's Wood, across the field, beyond the back of our wood, was more open with big trees, mature oak; chestnut and holly trees. We would mainly visit this wood in the autumn to collect chestnuts, and I had very sore fingers trying to get those nuts out of their prickly shells. Those chestnuts, walnuts and a few hazelnuts were the only nuts we had during the war and I don't recall other nuts even at Christmas time. Our mother made marzipan for the Christmas cake, using semolina and almond essence, (which put me off marzipan for years).

As we grew older, Nickley woods, across the road and three fields away from our house, was to become our favourite wood to roam in. We had not explored these particular woods until John became friends with a new boy that came to our school. I was in the lower end of the big classroom, when the headmaster appeared with two children and announced to the whole room; they were to be called Roy and Angela Hall. Roy was the same age as my brother and Angela was a year younger than me. This was the only time this ever happened and I have since wondered if they may have changed their surname because they were Jewish. Where they came from, I do not know, but they now lived in a little wooden house in the middle of Nickley Woods. Roy was sat next to John at school and they became friends. As our mother did not like John and me wandering in other woods on our own, I always went with John to Roy's house in the holidays. Their father was in the army and I saw him once or twice, when he came home on leave. Their mother was tall and wore long black clothes, and

Roy said that the locked house next door to them belonged to his grandparents, and we were not allowed in it. Though she was younger, Angela was bigger than me, and had a mass of ginger curls, falling in ringlets down her back. I did not like her very much; Roy was much nicer, she was always screaming if she did not get her own way, so, we called her Violet Elizabeth; a fictional girl from the 'Just William Books'. One summer holiday, their mother, as she was working, asked our mother if Roy and Angela could stay at our house during the day. Of course, she agreed, but later regretted it. As children, we would never think of going into our parents' bedroom and we had no reason to go into our bedrooms during the day either. Often, our mother found Angela wandering around the house, and then was told by Roy that she took things, so she was searched every time she went home. I remember the time that she packed a little tin with our Christmas pudding silver three penny bits, and tucked it up her knickers' leg. I think it was then my mother told Mrs Hall that it was too much of a responsibility to have the children full time, but we still had them to play and went to their house to play. I remember going to their house one day and spending ages looking for their mothers lost rings. I do not know if they were found.

There were quite a few houses down the grassy lane in Nickley Woods, some were lived in, and some were not. I particularly remember one house that was raised off the ground, with wooden steps leading up to a locked front door. So, one day we crept under the house and through a hole in the floor. We went into the kitchen, it was in a bit a mess with broken food packets and papers all over the floor, and I think animals may have been responsible. The table was laid, as if somebody had just walked out, in the middle of a meal. We explored the rest of the house and came across a dusty bedroom and a living room with an out-of-tune piano, which delighted my brother. After this, we would often go to this house for John to play the piano. Like my mother and Lesley, he could also play music by ear, and I was always very jealous of them. At the end of this lane, near the road, was a rather sinister, black wooden bungalow that was falling down. We were told a girl had been murdered there, but I was unsure how true that was.

Once, I went with our mother to an auction at a house that was being sold and she bought some kitchen knives there. It belonged to the family of a girl that was murdered and thrown down a well. There seemed to be some truth in this, because on the school bus, other children pointed out the house where the mother of the man who murdered the girl still lived. It happened before our parents had moved to the area, but my mother had been told that the man was mentally unstable and ended up in an asylum. As soon as the war ended, the Hall family disappeared. But, Nickley Woods, with its Chestnut trees, continued, for many years, to be our favourite place for gathering chestnuts.

The children we knew in the war years, like us, had very few toys; no televisions; videos; phones; CDs'; amusement parks and very limited money. There was just Children's Hour, at 5 o'clock every day, on the wireless. Pop songs were not played on the radio until many years after the war. Holidays were out of the question and all the sea sides near us were out of bounds, as they were mined and covered in barbed wire. The cinemas were open in Ashford, but we never went, because we were too young to go on our own, and the adults in the family were far too busy to take us. Living in the middle of Canterbury, and as an only child growing up in the war years, my husband told me, he was taken to the cinema two or three times a week by his mother and grandmother. Now, I consider myself incredibly fortunate to have spent my childhood at Oak Lodge and in the surrounding area, with an adventurous older brother, in such a fantastic natural playground.

As Auntie Vi and the boys spent a lot of time at our house, there was a well-worn track, with all the comings and goings, between Oak Lodge and Wood View. There was no pavement but, as cars were noisier and slower than today, on the straight bit of road, we had time to step on the verge as the traffic went by. My grandmother very seldom came to our house, but I went to their house to read books. It was always warm there, summer and winter, as the kitchen range, in the living room was always alight. My grandmother had been the cook in a big house and had spent most of her life cooking on kitchen ranges. She was a brilliant cook and very often, her dishes would come along the road for us to eat.

All the year round, the animals had to be fed and watered, nothing was wasted and all spare food was given to the animals. My aunt brought along their spare food and every morning the vegetable peelings were cooked in a big saucepan on a primus stove in the shed. The cooked vegetables were then mixed with a ground cereal, obtained with egg coupons, instead of eggs. I remember my mother giving a spoonful of this warm mash to the waiting dog. In winter, the rabbits were mainly fed on hay and dry bread, but as the weather became warmer, John and I were often asked to go and find some green stuff for them. All the animals had water bowls which had to be filled daily. Kitty Wee was the only cat we had during the war years; she was a great mouser and lived for about twenty years. Rags got run over on the road at the beginning of the war and was replaced with Binkie, a little Jack Russel. She had seven puppies, which my mother gave away. I can still visualise these puppies in a row, falling asleep one by one, on the fender in front of the fire. Then one day, Basil, the shepherd from the farm, came and chopped their tails off on the chopping block. Our mother later wished she had kept one of these puppies, as not long after, Binkie died of distemper. She was replaced by a big lurcher type dog, which did not last long because it was a sheep chaser and was shot. Next was a sheepdog called Sally, who was a great guard dog, but did not like men. This was a bit of a problem for our father when he came home on leave. We had this dog towards the end of the war, when our father was away longer, and she was killed on the road before he was demobbed. Buster, a black spaniel, was the next dog, and he lasted quite a few years, until, he too, was run over on the road. Our dogs were never tied up, or taken for walks, and had the freedom to wander wherever they wanted, but mostly they would just stay around the house or go on the road, much to my mother's annoyance, so she would chase them off it with the copper stick.

We knew spring was coming when my mother brought in the steps to climb into the attic, to open the windows at either end, and cover the floor with newspapers. This was because, every year, swallows nested up there. John and I were able to climb up the lavatory door, to get into the attic, to look at the baby birds in the nests, and sometimes John would take an egg. At this time of year, I would go miles with John, through woods, along hedgerows, looking for birds' nests. He had a bird book and knew every local bird and the shape and colour of their eggs. When we found a nest, he would take only one egg, if it was one he wanted for his collection, making sure it was fresh and not addled (a half grown chick inside). For the collection, the egg had to be blown; this meant making a small hole in the top and bottom of the egg with a needle, then blowing the contents out. The eggs were then stored on cotton wool, in an air tight tin, to stop the moths eating them. We would visit the nests we found, time and time again, until the baby birds had flown. If we found a nest with cold eggs, we knew it had been abandoned for some reason. We climbed trees and waded across ponds, but never came to any harm. One time, we found some round white eggs, without shells, under a bush, beside a pond, and my brother identified them as belonging to a snake. In the spring, we knew where the best places to pick primroses were and picked bunches for our family and the old ladies in our road. There were no chocolate Easter Eggs during the war, so our treat was to go to church with Aunty Vi, for the Easter service. We also went to church on Palm Sunday and were each given a cross made from a reed that came from Jerusalem, we were told.

The very few photographs I have of the family, during this time, were taken by Auntie Vi. She was the only one in the family with a camera, and Uncle Art occasionally managed to get a roll of film. This meant, taking a photograph had to be planned, with all of us together, usually in a row. This sometimes happened when we were all clean and dressed up, ready to go to Sunday School, at three o'clock in the afternoon. In the summer, dressing up for Sunday school was an inconvenience because it interrupted our play, but we went, to get enough stamps to go to the Christmas party. These parties, held by the Church, were the only ones we went to during the war. Mrs Meek, a retired school teacher, living in the house next door to our grandmother, held Sunday school, in her house, just for our family. She was a very regal lady, who wore dresses down to her ankles and black boots, one of which had a build-up heel and sole because she had a club foot. She told us about a visit to her son in Australia, taking six weeks to get there by boat. In her sitting room, where we sang hymns, accompanied by her on the piano, was a whole wall of books, which she allowed me to borrow.

We had unlimited access to all of our father's tools as long as we put them back. These included scythes, axes, pick axes, hammers and saws of all kinds. My brother made great guns out of planks of wood, and bows and arrows, and catapults. I learnt, very early in life, our father did not like anything to be left out at night. We cut down trees [not the big oak trees] and made camps, cut paths through the wood and every Summer holiday we dug a big hole at the top of the garden (because there, it was above the water table, and did not fill with water). The clay soil was very hard to dig, but did not collapse, so we could make steps down into the hole and cut out shelves in the sides. One hot and dry summer, we made some bowls, cups, plates and lots of animals out of the clay and dried them in the sun, which the little ones enjoyed playing with. Another year, we made all the items for a grocers shop out of the clay.

Using the hole, with sheets of corrugated iron over the top as a dugout, we took turns throwing lumps of dirt at it, or being in it with lumps of earth crashing on the tin roof. It was a favourite war game.

The Hole.

Chapter 6

A Corn Stook

During the war years, my time was spent between home and school. We did not go on holidays, and the first Christmas of the war, in Folkestone, was the only time I spent away from home. At the beginning of the war, our mother went on holiday and took Lesley, as a baby, to visit our father, who was stationed, at the time, in Buxton. Auntie Vi stayed to look after us. Very occasionally, I went shopping with my mother, in Ashford, sometimes to buy shoes, or for an eye hospital appointment in Maidstone. In most towns, a low brick wall topped with iron railings with an iron gate was the frontage of many houses. At the beginning of the war, these railings were sawn off, leaving rusting jagged pieces of iron on top of the walls. The railings and gates were taken away to help the war effort and never replaced. It was on one of those rare journeys into town, that I cut my finger on one of those jagged pieces of iron. It went septic and the poultice and iodine treatment did not work so I was taken to the doctor's surgery in Hamstreet, on the bus. There, he cut my finger open with a scalpel. I recall feeling very faint and my mother going to the butcher's, which was opposite the surgery. The next thing I knew, was being driven back home, in the back of the butcher's three wheeled van.

Directly, we got indoors and my mother treated the finger with a very hot poultice. She told me later, the doctor, without using any anaesthetic, cut my finger with a scalpel that was in a tray of dirty dressings. Two weeks later she learned that the doctor had committed suicide with a drug overdose. My mother said that he was a very handsome young man.

Another outing, in the holidays, was walking to the welfare in Hamstreet with our mother, Auntie Vi, brother, younger sisters, cousins and two prams. In those days, babies and children under five were weighed and checked over. If you did not attend those clinics, at least once a month, the District Nurse would turn up on the doorstep, so my mother said. Orange juice, milk powder and cod liver oil were available from the clinic. The orange juice we loved, but the cod liver oil was dreadful and we hated it. Our mother did not make us take it, but she put it in the chicken mash until the eggs started tasting of cod liver oil, then she stopped. The powdered milk was used to make lovely peppermint humbugs. Sometimes we did some shopping in the village and went to a small park, with a couple of swings and a see-saw then walked the two miles back home. As we walked along the road, in the spring, John looked for birds' nests in the hedgerows and in the autumn we picked blackberries. We had very few blackberry bushes in the grounds of Oak Lodge and the best blackberries were usually found in the hedges along the edges of the roads.

During the war, Harden's Farm played a very important part in our lives. Mr Harden was always there to help, and having access to the only phone in the area was a great asset. He gave both our mother and aunt seasonal jobs on the farm. They pecked thistles, hoed mangles, turned over hay and stoked corn. Auntie Vi spent more time on the farm than my mother because Nanna Beavis was looking after their house while our mother, on her own, had a bigger house and garden and more children to look after. We went with them during the school holidays, as extra hands were needed to help with harvesting the grain crops. The cut wheat, barley and oats were bound with twine and made into sheaves, which had to be stood up in blocks of eight for the grain to dry. This had to be done when the weather was right.

These were long days so, we took our lunch and the pram across the fields and the dog came too. Our lunches were not remarkable, but I do remember the men on the farm drinking cold tea, no milk or sugar, out of glass bottles. Sometimes, we were away from the house for many hours, and as the kitchen tap was our only access to water, we had to wait until we got home to have a drink. There were no plastic bottles of water and we never went to any restaurants or cafes during the war. Auntie Vi helped at threshing time and worked on the part of the farm where spiels were made. Spiels are posts made from chestnut poles stripped of their bark and used on the farm for gates and fencing. All the year round, we children roamed all over the farm, helping or hindering the work there. One of my favourite activities was to ride on the back of the trailer. The trailer was towed by a tractor, and had rubber tyres and a bar at the back that you could sit on; whether it was picking up hay or corn, we would follow this trailer round the fields for free rides. Other carts with wooden wheels, drawn by horses, with no bar at the back to sit on, were very bumpy to ride in. I remember how enjoyable it was to walk through a hay field at any time of the year, but fields cultivated with wheat, barley and oats were a different matter. In the spring, these fields were muddy, in the summer the crops grew taller than me, in the autumn when the crops were cut, it left sharp, stiff, stalks which scratched bare legs. I had no rubber boots, no trousers, and jeans were not around, so the best I could do was to wear long socks. John wore short trousers, so his legs got scratched as well. Because it was far too dangerous to go into a field while a crop was being cut, we sat on the gate to watch. The reaping machine, with a man sitting on it, towed by a tractor, would cut the corn and bundle it into sheaves. Starting at the edge of the corn field and cutting in strips, the machine went round and round, making the corn patch in the middle smaller and smaller, and then suddenly, rabbits would run out of the middle, across the field, to be shot at by the waiting men with guns. After the crop was harvested, we were allowed to collect the fallen heads of grain to give to our chickens back home.

Every afternoon the farmer would open the gate by the field with the cows in, and walk back to the farm. On their own, the cows would slowly come across the field, out the gate, up the main road, into the farm yard, to their own particular stall in the cow shed. I watched the cows being milked by hand, in the dusty cow sheds, with the pink cow licks on the wall. You would always find a cat or two asleep, and chickens wandering around. I collected eggs in all sorts of strange places, and in the spring it was not unusual to see a hen with chicks wandering about. There were about twelve milking cows, each named, each a different shape and colour. The cows must have been milked very early in the morning, for it to be delivered to us to have fresh milk for breakfast, before going to school. Auntie Vi worked in the dairy and sometimes I went with her and watched what happened to the afternoon milk.

The milk was poured through a muslin cloth into large round bowls and left for the cream to settle on the top. This was then scooped off, with a special scoop, into a wooden churn, with a handle that was turned for ages before the cream turned to butter. My mother was the only one who liked this butter; to me it tasted a bit odd. At the end of each day, any milk, skimmed milk, or butter milk left over was fed to the pigs. The morning milking happened early in the day, while I was asleep, but the cows mooed at the gate in the afternoons if the farmer was late opening it. In another field, there was a herd of brown cows and calves, and sometimes a bull with ring in its nose; we were always very careful to watch where that bull was, before crossing that field.

In the farmyard, raised off the ground, was a big barn with wooden steps leading up to a wide door, and I would often see the farmer's son sitting on these steps. He was older than us, and I cannot remember seeing him around the farm very much. On the back of the barn, in the sunshine, were a couple of ferrets in cages. These were a dirty, yellow-white in colour and smelt dreadful. When we poked their cages with a stick, they would fly to the front of the cage to attack us with their yellow teeth and pink eyes. Ferrets were used to catch rabbits, but I never saw these out of the cages. Food for the animals was kept in the big barn where there was a machine with a big wheel that chopped up mangles (sugar beet). Next to the barn was a round house which sometimes housed a bull, this also stank. Next to that was a black shed, which was the home of the local tramp. He lived there and was fed by the farmer's wife, who left his food on the step outside. Every day he walked down the middle of the road pushing a two-wheeled roadman's cart, swearing and talking to himself. We kept our distance because he also stank. We did not see him around after the war. In the field, next to his hut, was a big, long, dung heap where we dug for worms to go fishing, and in the summer, this stank. The pig sties, which were near the farm house, did not stink at all and I loved it when we were allowed to pick up the piglets. In the autumn, John and I collected acorns for these pigs, some years there were lots and other years very few.

The Hill family, who we visited on the hill before the war, had now moved to a cottage at Sugar Loaf cross roads. Mr Hill looked after Mr Harden's horses in the stables, at the back of the cottage. As we were about the same age, their daughter, Doris, and I became friends. She was a very pretty child, with peaches and cream complexion and a mass of long blond curls; sometimes in plaits. She would often come to our house on her little bike, a black replica of an adult bike, which she was very possessive about and would never let anybody else ride. I would walk to her house, or as I had no bike of my own, sometimes borrowed my mother's bike and rode it standing up on the pedals. I often had tea with Doris in their garden using a lovely children's tea set. I went to lovely parties there, attended by all her aunts, uncles and cousins, (most of them in our age group). My mother told me that Mrs Hill wanted Doris to be an only child, as she, herself, came from a very large family. Doris had aunts and uncles younger than she was, and once we visited this large family that lived near Ashford. Doris and I spent time with her father in the stables with the three cart horses that lived there. By far the biggest, was Captain, a chestnut brown shire horse with white fluffy hooves. Violet was a gentle, dark brown cart horse. Tom, another cart horse, was unpredictable, so we gave him a wide berth. Some years later, he died when his heart burst while pulling a cart. One day, Mr Hill put me on Captain's back, and Doris on Violet's back, and we rode the mile down the road to the Blacksmith's in Hamstreet for the horses to be shod. Then we rode all the way back to the stables. I saw these horses working at hay-making time and harvesting time, but I do not know what they did for the rest of the year. Doris remained the only child in her family, so it was very tragic when at the age of eighteen, she died of throat cancer.

During the war years, home, family, friends, school, and very little beyond, was my whole world, which was all roughly within a five mile radius. At that time, I had very little understanding of how dangerous war was, of cities being bombed and many people being killed. All I knew was to carry my gas mask at all times. Many times, when playing, I forgot it on purpose, but I always took it to school. When the village siren went off (a wavy note for danger) while at school, we would go into the bomb shelter, and when the siren sounded the all clear (a single note for safety), we came out and went back into the classrooms. At home, we had no siren, so were told, at the sound of planes approaching, to get in the house, or if we were away from the house, to get in a ditch or shelter under the trees, but never to stay in open ground. Whenever we could, John and I watched any activity in the sky from wherever we could get the best view, which was always in the open, and our mother was always shouting at us to get indoors. As we had no shelter until the time of the Doodlebugs, my mother made us sit in the passage, behind the kitchen door, as she thought this was the safest place in the house. She was wrong.

It was a good thing I enjoyed going to school, because our mother would never allow us to stay at home unless we were really ill. In those days, when I was at the Primary School, children progressed through the school according to ability not age. In the infants' class we were given slates and chalks, learnt the alphabet, numbers, and how to knit. Before leaving this class, a child had to be able to write their name, read a simple book and know the two times' table. In the next class, we were given pencils and paper, and modelled with plasticine (I remember an older boy in the class making beautiful plasticine models). For mental arithmetic, the whole class stood up, and when a child answered a question correctly, they sat down. We had to know the three to six times' tables, before progressing to the big room which held the next class and the top class. In the next class, the desks had inkwells and we were given pens with nibs and blotting paper. There, we had lessons in joined up writing with loops. I had trouble using the awful pens and the ink was awful too, which meant blots and blue fingers. In this class, we had painting lessons using a paint box with just three colours: red, yellow and blue and the teacher would come along and squeeze some white paint out of a tube onto the lid. In this class, the girls had a sewing lesson one afternoon a week while the boys played football. In the girls' playground, we played hopscotch, skipping and ball games but never any competitive games. The big classroom had a high wooden ceiling, peppered with paper sails attached to pen nibs; I never saw any thrown. The windows were too high to see out of, and the whole room was heated by a big coke stove in the middle of the room and a small round coke stove by Mrs Darton's desk. This room held two classes; the lower class taught by Mrs Darton and the top class taught by Mr Ainsworth, the headmaster. Badly behaved boys were lined up by his desk, then with one foot on a small chair; he would put a boy across his knee, pull the boys trousers tight across his bottom and whack him once or twice with a thin cane.

The girls, he hit across the hand with a ruler. This headmaster often sang to me, 'Beautiful dreamer awake unto me', because I was always day dreaming. In his last term at primary school, I sat next to John, near the back of the classroom. In this class, we were allowed to walk to the village in the lunch hour and occasionally I went with John to buy wooden tops, marbles, cap bombs and round boxes of caps. One day, while I was in this classroom, a very sick little boy came in from another part of the school and was laid on some desks that were pushed together, in front of the stove. He lay there very still, for a long time, before he was taken away and later we heard he had died.

During the war, we found many ways to amuse ourselves. Balls were extremely difficult to come by and were soon lost in our large garden. Mrs

Wilson, next door, gave us a croquet set, a game we became quite expert at playing. We also developed a rather dangerous version of cricket with the croquet balls. We had some tennis rackets that belonged to our father but as we had no tennis balls, the only use we had for them was to intercept Maybugs as they flew south to north through our garden, once a year. On November the fifth, there were no fireworks until well after the war ended, so we just made a big bonfire. Running around the wood with sparks flying off lighted sticks was the nearest we got to fireworks. We ended up roasting chestnuts on a piece of tin laid on the embers of the dying fire. This was followed by chicken soup, made from an old laying hen, and toffee apples made by our mother.

As food was rationed, our mother knew the amount of basic ingredients allocated to our family and planned the meals around them. = We had sandwiches for lunch, and our mother always cooked dinner at tea time when we came in from school. Because electricity was very expensive, when my mother had the electric oven on, she filled it up. We had roast dinners with Yorkshire puddings, on Sundays, casseroles with dumplings; rabbit stew; steak and kidney pudding; liver and bacon; shepherd's pie; baked potatoes; sage and onion stuffed hearts and very occasionally, chicken. For desserts, we had all sorts of steamed puddings; milk puddings; bread and butter pudding; bread pudding; apple and other fruit pies; baked apples; strewed rhubarb and pancakes. We had some homemade cakes; jam tarts; buns; scones and sponges, but biscuits were bought from the shop. I did not like biscuits, ginger cake, fizzy drinks or fish paste. I liked toast; the bread was toasted under the grill and sometimes on a toasting fork in front of the fire. The toast was mainly spread with dripping and marmite, seldom with butter, as the ration was very small. The Sunday roast always produced a bowl of dripping, and my favourite for toast was pork dripping. We made toffee, fudge and sweets. We had no fridge, so in the summer, our mother put the butter, margarine, lard and cheese in a bucket and lowered it down the well to keep cool. Any milk left at the end of the day, was boiled, because otherwise it would be sour by the next morning. We were very lucky to have a big vegetable garden and we were self-sufficient, mainly in potatoes; runner beans; apples and eggs. Local people, with spare produce, would put a 'for sale' notice on their gates and our mother and aunt would go off, on their bikes, and come back with bags of fruit and vegetables, some of which they bottled or made into jam with some of the sugar ration. We would go blackberry picking and Mr Harden allowed us to pick the fruit from the damson hedge by the farm. The shelves in the larder were stacked with pots of jam, Kilmer jars full of fruit, a bucket with eggs in a liquid Izanglass! And stone jars filled with runner beans in salt. Wooden trays of apples were kept under a bed, which made the room smell very nice. Sometimes cooked food was put in the larder; away from the flies, with cooked beetroot in vinegar, away from Kitty Wee, who with her paw, hooked slices out of the bowl and ate them. As the larder was quite large, with lots of shelves, our few toys were kept in there as well. In the autumn, we knew where mushrooms could be found. I loved mushrooms, particularly when our mother cooked them, in the oven, in butter and milk. Both she and John were allergic to mushrooms, but he enjoyed picking them and she cooked them for us.

Sometimes, mice would come into the house after food, but Kitty Wee was a very good mouser, so they did not last long. I saw mice in the house, but never any rats, although I sometimes saw them in the sheds. The family increased to five children when Jacky was born in September 1943. John left the Primary School to go to a school in Ashford. His friend Roy Hall went to the Grammar School as a fee paying pupil. My mother wished that she had paid for John to go to the Grammar School, because a couple of years later, the fee paying stopped, and all the children that were already there, stayed and continued their education for free. Every morning, in my last year at the primary school, Valerie and I would wait for 'The Tub', outside my aunt's house, and when it came, she would drag Michael down the path and throw him on the bus. It was my job to keep him on the bus and take him into school. Many times I was called out of my class to deal with him in the infants' class.

As far back as I can remember, the bungalows in our row were never empty for long, as fast as one family moved out, another moved in. In the year before my last year at primary school, Mrs Barrett and her four daughters moved into

Selvin Wood, the house next door but one, to us. The eldest, Mrs Mc Kay (Mr McKay was in the army) came with her two children, Bobby and Vera, who were about the same age as my sisters. Next was Gladys, married to Reg (who was in the forces), then came Louise, who had just left school and worked in Ashford. The youngest was a very pretty girl, who was a year older than me, called Florry. She came to the primary school for just one year and we became friends.

OntheFarm

Daddy, Avril
John, Michael, Auntie Sybil, Valerie,
Buster, Lesley, Jacky, Robin, Peter. 1946

Oak Lodge after the War.
Facing away from the house
Towards the Wood

Avril at Grammar School

Jacky, Lesley, Valerie and Avril.

Avril at Primary School

Chapter 7

In the Morrison Shelter

During the first four years of the war, cities all around Britain were bombed and many people were killed, but all this had very little effect on my life, until the final year of the war, when the situation changed dramatically. First the Americans arrived, causing a lot more activity on the roads and in the sky. Long American convoys went by the house and camps were set up in the forest, with guns and vehicles covered with camouflage netting, concealed amongst the trees. Small local airfields were taken over by the Americans, which meant even more activity in the sky and more planes for my brother to identify. Once, after watching a dog fight in the sky, we saw a couple of parachutes float out of a plane trailing black smoke. A plane appeared from nowhere, and as I could hear the cracks of gun fire, and see by red streaks from its wings, it was firing at the parachutes. On another day, I vividly remember seeing a row of black soldiers sitting on the five bar gate opposite our house, and another group playing dice in the middle of the road. When they saw us, they smiled, their teeth looked very white against their black faces and Valerie and Lesley ran indoors. They had never seen a black man before.

Often, when the American convoys went by our house, we would stand on the edge of the road, hoping, if we were lucky, to get chewing gum and sweets thrown at us. Until, on one particular day, Valerie ran into the road in front of a jeep, to pick up some sweets and to avoid running over her, the jeep screeched to a halt, which had a knock on effect on the rest of the convoy. Our mother came rushing out of the house when she heard the noise, and was very cross, and from then on, made us stand behind the gate. John and I were not very pleased with Valerie as begging for sweets from that place was less effective. All this activity was the build-up for D-Day (Operation Overlord). On another occasion, an American convoy stopped along the edge of our road and a jeep, with a fixed machine gun in the back and towing a very posh small caravan, parked in our drive. I think he might have been a General, and he allowed my brother to sit in the machine gun seat and showed us the inside of the caravan. It was there for several days and my mother washed some of his clothes, which she said, were far superior to those issued to my father. When we came in from school, chocolate and sweets were left on the dresser for us. I woke up one morning and they had all disappeared, and our American General had left behind some clothes and a kit bag, which hung around the wash house for years. After the Americans left, John and I went into the forest and found big heaps of disposable petrol cans, and in one of these cans, we found a quantity of pennies and halfpennies, which we kept secret from our mother. Later, I was told that the Americans did not like carrying these low value coins around in their pockets. I cannot remember what we spent the money on, but it was not sweets.

It was about the time that the Americans arrived, that, first Aunty Vi, then John and I, and finally my mother, caught Yellow Jaundice (Hepatitis !), later in life, this stopped us all being blood donors. Valerie also had a mystery illness and lost the use of her legs. She was six at the time but I remember her in a cot in the kitchen and my mother massaging her legs and eventually getting her to walk again. She had lost a lot of weight, so when she went back to school, was given the nick-name 'faggots', because she was so thin. My mother blamed the Americans for these illnesses and later wondered if Valerie had contracted polio.

Our father came home in the spring of 1944 to plant the potatoes, but could not dig them up in the autumn as he was abroad at that time, so we had to dig them up. I suppose we were lucky because our father, a sergeant in the army, stayed in this country until he went to France on D-Day. He was part of the D-Day invasion force and ended up landing on Juno Beach with the Canadians. Once, he told me that he always tried to carry a small spade and a small sheet of corrugated iron, so he could dig a hole, get in it, and cover it with the corrugated iron. He stayed fighting in Europe for the rest of the war, ending up in Belgium on V.E. Day. He got a recommendation from General Montgomery, and this hung in a frame, on the wall, for years. He did not talk much about his time in France, but I do remember a story about a pie. Apparently, he and his mates made a big pie using tins of corn beef and pastry made from ships biscuits smashed up with a hammer. They made an oven out of bricks, lit a fire underneath and put the pie in. They were being shelled at the time, so went to a shelter, but when they came out, an unexploded shell had landed on the pie oven and smashed it to bits, so all their hard work had been for nothing. He said that if the shell had exploded, they would all have been blown up.

After D-Day, a big map of Europe came with the newspaper; this John put on the wall, and put pins in it to record the movement of the forces; according to the news on the radio or in the newspapers as they advanced through Europe. After he was evacuated, it was my job to carry on, until he came home.

While D-Day is a blur, I have a vivid memory of the first Doodlebugs that came over our house in the middle of the night (I have since learnt, it was about four in the morning). We were all woken up by planes flying low with a strange engine noise. My mother went outside, in the dark, and could not make any sense

72

of the strange small planes with flames coming out of the back. At first, she thought it was a plane crashing, but when another one came, from the same direction, then another, she changed her mind. We, all five kids, got into her bed and stayed there for the rest of the night. There was no information on the news or in the newspapers for the next few days. Eventually we learned that they were unmanned flying bombs on their way to London. The V1 (Vergeltungswaffen 1), a vengeance weapon, was launched by the Germans one week after the successful allied landings in Normandy. At the peak, over 100 a day were fired over South East England, 9251 in total. 4261 were destroyed before they reached London; many over the sea. The numbers got less and less by October, when the last launch pad within range was destroyed by the allied forces; the flying bombs no longer flew over us. They continued to be launched from planes and sites in Germany to places in France and Belgium where the troops were fighting. They were nick-named 'Doodlebugs' because of the unusual sound they made. I did not realise, at the time, quite how unsafe it was to be living in the South East of England, where planes were shot down, and then flying bombs were shot down before they ran out of fuel and fell out of the sky on London.

Because of all this activity going on in our area, we had an indoor Morrison shelter set up in our living room. It was the size of a double bed and the height of a table, with a solid sheet of steel on the top, bed springs on the bottom, and removable wire frames on all four sides. We slept sideways in this shelter, as there were too many of us to fit in the normal way: John, me, Valerie, Lesley, Jacky and then our mother in a row. Some of us had our feet sticking out, so on one side, the wire frame was opened up and leaned against the wall. When our mother got into bed, she closed the wire frame on her side. If there was any activity in the night, in order to put the wire frame at the bottom down, she would say, "pull your feet up", and we would all do so, in our sleep. During the daytime, the side of the shelter was left open so that we could get in there in a hurry.

It was about this time that children were being evacuated from our area and our mother decided that John and I should go. She packed all the clothes on the list in our suit cases. Some she had to buy, and clothes were difficult to find, so I was bought a large pair of pink knickers, which I never wore. I believe Valerie had them in the end, because she loved big knickers that came up to her armpits. It was the summer holidays and we were evacuated to a flat above a fire station in the middle of Torquay. It was so different; John and I wandered about the streets and round the harbour, caught crabs with pieces of bread on strings and went swimming in the swimming pool. After two weeks, I had to go back home because I had won a scholarship to the Grammar School and would lose my place if I stayed away. I came back on the train, on my own, under the supervision of the guard, and was met in London by Auntie Elsie who put me in the guard's van to Ashford, where I was met by my mother. John stayed in Torquay, spent one term at school there, and was home for Christmas.

Doodlebugs always followed the same path, unless they were damaged by gunfire and flew off course. On one occasion, I saw one returning the way it had come. We always dreaded seeing a plane in the sky with a Doodlebug because it would try and shoot it down, or fly very close, to tip the wing, to make it go off course. It was always a great relief when the Doodlebug had flown over without the engine cutting out, not even realising it had to come down, causing destruction somewhere. One day, during the school holidays, Auntie Vi was working on the farm and we were all down in the fields near Sugar Loaf helping with the threshing. Our mother was at home with Jacky, and Nanna Beavis was at her house, looking after Robin. It was a lovely summer day and there were no planes in the sky. Suddenly, a Doodlebug came silently, low over the trees, crashed and blew up in the direction of where our bungalows stood. John and Auntie Vi, with Lesley in the seat on the back, jumped on their bicycles and raced home. I was left to walk, with Valerie and Michael, the mile along the road back home. The Doodlebug had blown up very close to the end bungalow, demolishing it completely. The old man that lived there was injured, taken away and we never saw him again. The bungalow was left in ruins for many years and the bomb crater became a pond. The Doodlebug destroyed our conservatory, and some of our sheds collapsed like a pack of cards. Some of the kitchen windows were blown in, and the broken glass was mixed up with the contents of the dresser and the food cupboards. The kitchen windows were replaced with pieces of roofing felt, which my mother opened each day and secured with a hammer and nail.

I remember vividly the day another Doodle Bug exploded at the edge of our wood.

The Doodlebugs always came from the same direction, and on that day, I first heard the sound of one approaching, and watched it, as it came from the usual direction, over the trees.

Suddenly, a twin engine aircraft appeared from the left, with its guns firing at it, the engine stopped, and I saw it heading straight for our house. I ran indoors, into the Morrison shelter and waited. There was a huge explosion, followed by the tinkling of glass and then complete silence. Our mother had gone to get Jacky, who was asleep in the pram in the garden. She was crossing the kitchen, when the blast blew the glass (from the surviving window in the kitchen) into her legs. She was taken to the hospital with Jacky, Auntie Vi and Robin, and they were there for hours. John and I took Valerie and Lesley to our grandmother and then went back through our wood to explore the bomb site; on the way noticing loads of leaves and branches everywhere. There was no hole in the ground, as the flying bomb had exploded in the tree tops, making a perfect bowl-shaped hole in the wood. If it had not blown up in the tree tops, it would have exploded nearer, or on our house. We were the first ones there, and amongst the smoking debris we found a huge metal ball made of wire. It was still too hot to touch, but as it had a hole through the middle, we found a branch to move it, when it cooled down. While we were waiting, the Americans appeared and put our branch through the hole in our ball and walked off with it. They struggled with the weight, so I think we may have had a problem. Later, we were told that it was the first whole wire ball that had been found. What they did not find, was the tail piece the bit flames came out of, as this had landed in the middle of our wood, away from the rest of the wreckage. It was far too heavy to move and lay there, for many years, until it rusted away. Also, in later years, pieces of shrapnel were found in the trunks of our trees, when sawing them into logs. We were told to leave the site, so we went back and sat in the ditch outside my grandmother's house, where we were told a food van was coming because our kitchen was in such a mess. It never came, so we shared a rice pudding which had been cooking in Nanna Beavis's kitchen range and had escaped the soot which had fallen down the chimney.

When the Doodlebug came down in our wood, it blew the kitchen door off its hinges, down the passage, smack against the wall where we used to sit in supposed safety before we had the Morrison shelter. This explosion lifted the roof, one side of the house moved out, and daylight could be seen through the front room ceiling. As the house was made of wood, the builders just lifted the roof and pushed the wall back in. Later that year, a second vengeance weapon was launched, the V-2, a rocket fired directly at London. For some time, it was kept a secret from the people. This weapon had very little effect on us.

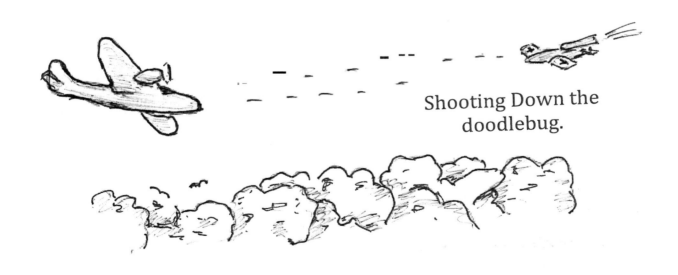

Shooting Down the doodlebug.

Chapter 8

Me off to Grammar School.

I have often thought how difficult the last year of the war must have been for my mother. My father was fighting in France, John was evacuated in Torquay, I went on the bus to school in Ashford, my two sisters went to school in Hamstreet and she was left at home with Jacky as a baby. The war was the reason my aunt and grandmother moved near my mother and they were there for each other for the rest of their lives. Until now, I have never given a thought as to how my father, a great family man, coped through all the years he was away from us. As far as I can remember, the last year of the war was a very exciting time for me, but it did have an adverse effect on my two younger sisters. Valerie developed a twitch, a constant blinking of the eyes, for which she was given glasses. Lesley, whenever there was the sound of a plane or Doodlebug, would turn round and round on the same spot screaming. My mother was always shouting to us, "Get Lesley". It was about this time that our mother started smoking, and continued to smoke until her grandchildren came along. My father had always smoked and never gave it up.

In the year John went to secondary school, he was evacuated. I began my education at the County School, as it was then called. I knew nobody there, as only one girl and one boy were given a scholarship from Hamstreet Primary School each year. Over half the children in my first year at this school were fee paying pupils, or came from fee paying schools, and were far more advanced in their education. It took me, at least a couple of years, to catch up. Some of the girls had already played tennis, hockey, netball and rounders, and I had only played football and cricket with my brother. There were writing lessons, where I was made to change from joined-up writing with loops, which I had been taught, to joined-up writing without loops, which is the way I write today. I enjoyed going to this school as it was always lovely and warm; even the cloakrooms and toilets had central heating. For the first time, I had school dinners instead of sandwiches. The food was served in dishes to tables with ten girls, two of whom were sixth formers. The head of the table served the main dish and we helped ourselves to vegetables. Glasses and a jug of water were placed on each table and Grace was said before every meal. I liked the different rooms and teachers for each subject.

Catching the earliest bus did not get me to school in time for assembly, so I would wait outside the hall with the other late comers for it to finish before we all filed in for the notices. We still had shelter practices, but this time the shelters were underground, in the playing fields, where in one far corner was an artillery gun post. On my bus journey to school, we passed a prisoner of war camp and occasionally we passed groups of P.O.W.'s marching along the road. I was told that they were Italian and they were all dressed alike; in clothes covered in different coloured patches. On one occasion, a P.O.W. came to my school and gave a music recital.

On the stage, surrounded by red velvet curtains, he played beautiful music on the grand piano, dressed in the P.O.W. clothes, covered in patches. Towards the end of the war, there were two German P.O.W.s working on the farm. The short stocky one, called Fritz, who was always laughing and smiling, eventually married a local girl and stayed in England after the war ended. Peter, the other, was tall and blond, very serious, seldom smiled and eventually went back to Germany.

The old prams given to us to play with were very useful in all sorts of ways. We would take the pram body off, just leaving the frame with the wheels. When John and I took the younger children through the woods, we would also take the pram wheels with a box on top. With one of us at the back, pushing, and one at the front, pulling with a piece of rope; it was the best vehicle for negotiating through the woods and fields. The children would take turns to ride in the box, with a pair of my father's rubber boots. When we came to a dyke, my brother would put on the boots and carry the children across, then drag the pram wheels across. He would throw the boots back to me, so I could cross the dyke, and we could carry on our way. On summer evenings, there were nightingales high in the sky, and bats flying around the house. Sometimes, on hot summer days, we sat on the road popping tar bubbles and occasionally saw a five inch long, smooth, orange caterpillar travelling, quite quickly, down the road; I only ever saw these caterpillars on the road. One day, when the farmer was delivering the milk, he noticed a hornets' nest in the corner of the house. He told my mother that they were dangerous with children around and said, as he kept bees, he would remove it. He gave us the beautifully constructed shaped cone nest, made of fine paper, which he had removed from the corner of the attic.

Towards the end of the war, more and more items could only be obtained with coupons. I remember my mother telling me that people were prepared to pay high prices for clothing coupons, and that she sold enough coupons to buy some sheets, which were very expensive. She gave tea coupons to my aunt and grandmother, who were big tea drinkers, as were their boys. In our house, at the time, my brother and I were the only tea drinkers and we had tea coupons for six people, (I think babies also got tea coupons). Both my aunt and grandmother received pensions and my aunt worked on the farm, so they were relatively well off. Ever so often, the growing boys were dressed from head to toe from the War Widows Fund; this was a great help. The soldiers pay at the beginning of the war was poor, so my mother struggled. As the war went on, the pay went up and our mother managed to have some savings. When our father was demobbed in 1945, he went to the Labour Exchange to sign on for a job; they employed him and he stayed with the Ministry of Labour, working in different locations until he retired. To begin with, I remember my mother saying, his wages were four pounds and ten shillings a week, which was less than the army pay, so my mother's one hundred pounds savings were taken out at the rate of two pounds a week until my father got a pay increase. It was difficult to make ends meet for some years after the war, with my father at home and us children growing up fast. There were shortages everywhere, even bread became rationed.

Aunty Vi, and particularly her boys, spent a great deal of time at our house.

Sometimes, after my sisters had been washed and put to bed, my mother washed Michael and he would wait for his mother to fetch him, to go home. The boys called my mother Auntie Lily, but because they had no father, always called my father 'Dadda Jack'. I do not remember when the war ended, but on V.E. (Victory in Europe) day, I do remember walking down a road somewhere, thinking, I am now living in peacetime. But the war was not over until two atom bombs were dropped on two cities in Japan, and the Japanese surrendered, and that was called V.J. (Victory in Japan) day. After peace was declared, we all went to a big celebration tea party in the village and my brother and I were sent back to the fire station in Torquay for a holiday. After spending two weeks revisiting all our old haunts, we came back on the train and it was a big surprise, to be met in London, by my recently demobbed father. We met up with Aunty Elsie and Uncle Billy for a very posh dinner somewhere. I was eleven years old and a waiter pulled out a chair, motioned me to stand in front of the table, and then pushed the chair in, for me to sit on. He picked up a table napkin, flicked it open, placed it in my lap, and then stood behind my chair. As I was sitting there feeling very grand with my hands under the table, a large piece of chewing gum fell into my hand. I was mortified, in case the waiter might think it was mine. I have no idea how I disposed of it. It was lovely to see my father and having him back for good, we were a real family again. I was particularly pleased as everybody always told me that I was his favourite. Within a few weeks of coming home, he bought me a bicycle.

Although I did appreciate peacetime, it made very little difference to my life; food was still rationed, and everything was in short supply, including money. It took a long time before things got back to normal. A plaque with Uncle Manuel's name on it, and two other names, was put on the wall in Orlestone Church. The men came back from the war to work on the farm, and the women were no longer needed. Our mother was too busy helping our father with the garden, and Aunty Vi got a job working in the farmhouse. John continued to be paid to work on the farm in the holidays, until he left school and joined the Air force. For years he got paid for shutting up Mr Wyatt's chickens on Sundays, which I very often helped him with. Mr Wyatt looked after his hundreds of chickens while Mrs Wyatt worked in London from Monday to Friday. At weekends, on Sunday evenings, they walked to the Pub in Hamstreet, which meant the chickens had to be shut up after it got dark. I would have loved to have had a paying job, but I was always expected to work for nothing, because I was a girl! All my working life, there was one pay scale for men and another, lower, pay scale for women, for doing the same job.

The two Doodlebugs that blew up near us, caused quite a lot of damage to the house and out buildings, so, after he was demobbed, our father arranged for all the repairs to the house to be done before the winter set in. He repaired the garage, workshops, and mended the iron shed. He started tidying up the garden which had become overgrown, as he had been abroad from D-day until he was demobbed after V.J. Day, which was over a year. In the following years, I spent a lot of time in the garden with my father, and in the winter, together we would choose seeds from a catalogue. These were mainly vegetables and a small selection of flower seeds, mainly annuals. In those days, my father made the seed boxes, and sieved his own compost, as there were no shops or garden centres to buy plants from. I remember, one year we grew about forty boxes of plants; the flower beds that year were quite spectacular. One long hot summer, after the war, we asked him if we could have a swimming pool and he said, "You dig it and I'll cement it". We started digging and made quite a big trench that summer holiday, but before we could finish, it was time to go back to school and the trench filled with water. As usual, my father put rubbish in it and filled it in. But in place of the swimming pool he made a tennis court which was played on for many years; by us and future generations.

In this book I have included my pre-war experiences to indicate the big difference the war made to my family and other families. My naïve childhood impression of the war years is probably very different to that of more understanding adults. Children visiting Oak Lodge over the years were motivated, in their interest in the war, by the wreckage of the Doodlebug in the wood.

Daddy, Mummy, John, Avril, Valerie, Lesley, Jacky, Buster and Peter.

The Victory Tea Party in Hamstreet.

Epilogue

Since writing this book, I realise that I never questioned my parents as to the reason they bought Oak Lodge all those years ago. Why my father who grew up in the middle of London, and my mother who grew up in the middle of Folkestone, moved to a house in the middle of the countryside, I will never know. I admire them for all their hard work, making Oak Lodge a memorable place to visit and for children to grow up in. The fourteen grandchildren often talk about spending many happy times there. Finally, after fifty years, in 1981, relatives, friends, children, grandchildren and one great grandchild were all there for their golden wedding party in the grounds of Oak Lodge.

The End

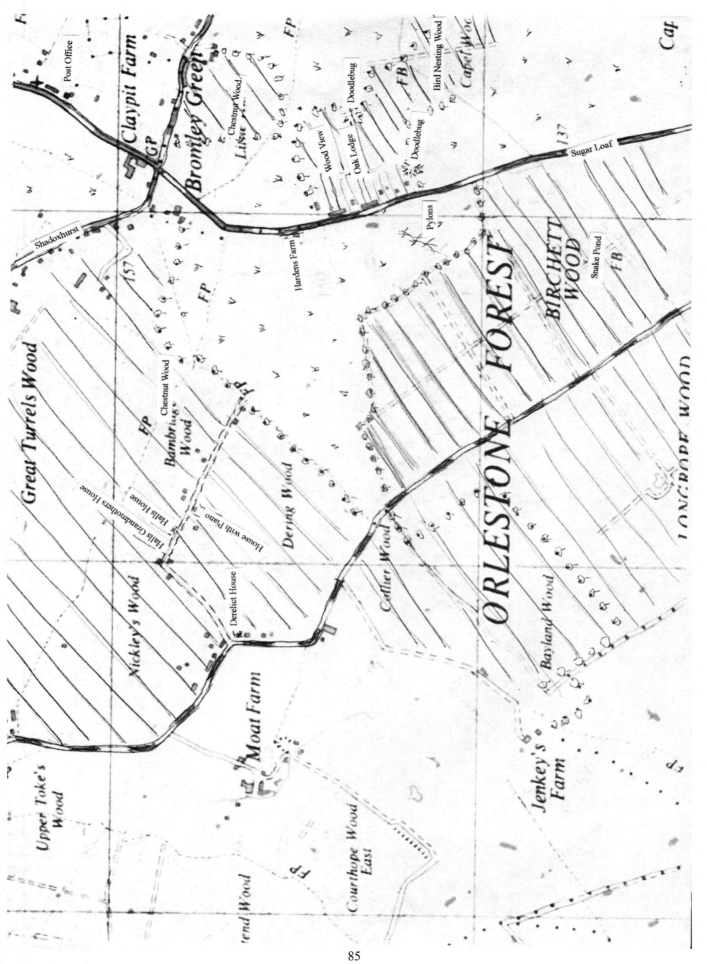